BRAINS AND PEOPLE

WILLIAM S. ROBINSON

Brains
and
People

An Essay on Mentality

and Its Causal Conditions

TEMPLE UNIVERSITY PRESS

PHILADELPHIA

Temple University Press, Philadelphia 19122
Copyright © 1988 by Temple University. All rights reserved
Published 1988
Printed in the United States of America

The paper used in this publication meets the minimum requirements of American
National Standard for Information Sciences—Permanence of Paper for Printed
Library Materials, ANSI Z39.48-1984

LIBRARY OF CONGRESS
Library of Congress Cataloging-in-Publication Data
Robinson, William S. (William Spencer), 1940–
    Brains and people: an essay on mentality and its causal conditions/William S.
Robinson.
        p. cm.
    Includes index.
    ISBN 0-87722-548-6 (alk. paper):
    1. Mind and body. 2. Cognition. I. Title.
BF161.R68   1988
128'.2—dc19   87-32174
                                                                          CIP

However, after all this has been said, I confess to a residual embarrassment. There is something in common between having an after-image and seeing a misprint. Both are visual affairs. How ought we to describe their affinity with one another, without falling back on to some account very much like a part of the orthodox theories of sense-impressions? To this I am stumped for an answer.

Gilbert Ryle

They liked to have books filled with things that they already knew, set out fair and square with no contradictions.

J. R. R. Tolkien

PREFACE

The aim of this book is to present people to themselves in such a way as to make it intelligible to them who and what they are. Having such an aim presupposes believing that there is some problem about understanding ourselves. One such problem gives rise to the organizational plan of this book. This problem is whether people are wholly and entirely physical things. There are four main, non-theological arguments that suggest that people are not wholly physical, and I discuss each of these in turn. It will be helpful if I begin by briefly describing these arguments and indicating in very broad terms what the outcome of the discussion of them will be.

The first argument concludes that people are not wholly physical because they have sensations and sensations cannot intelligibly be held to be composed of physical things. I believe that the premises of this argument can be articulated in such a way as to make them defensible and I explain how to do this in Chapter I. This stance brings me into conflict with much recent work on related issues. These issues are bound together by the fact that they all have something to do with claims about certainty, and I relate them to each other and to my view about sensations in Chapter II.

The second argument that sometimes convinces people that they are not wholly physical is based on the fact that their utterances have intentionality, that is, are *about* things. I do not believe that there can be a successful version of this argument. In Chapter III, I argue for a contrary view, namely that intentionality can be accounted for in an essentially physicalistic way. This account has enough affinities with behaviorism that it is natural to raise against it an old argument having to do with circularity in the assigning of beliefs and desires. I discuss this problem at length and explain how it is to be solved. To understand fully the strength of the account of Chapter III, however, it is necessary to understand why alternatives to it fail. The relevant alternatives include some physicalistic accounts as well as non-physicalistic ones. I address these alternatives in Chapter IV.

The third argument seeks to introduce a non-physical element as something required by the fact that it is we, our selves, who have our sensations, feelings, images, and thinkings. I do not believe that this can be made into a successful line of thought. In Chapter V, I present an account of the unity of the self that exhibits how the questions surrounding this topic can be answered without introducing any non-physical elements except those that can be introduced by the same argument that was developed in Chapter I.

The fourth argument introduces the non-physical on the ground that purely physical beings could not be proper subjects of ethical evaluation, as we people clearly are. Once again, I do not think this line of thought can be made to yield any non-physical requirement over and above what can be introduced by the argument of Chapter I. In the course of making this clear in Chapter VI, I confront the traditional problem of free will and also raise—and solve—a problem for contractualist ethics.

My method in examining these four arguments involves considering the work of many other philosophers. Part of the purpose of these discussions is often the criticism of some argument or the rejection of some claim. It seems appropriate, therefore, that I should warn the reader that my critical discussions are almost always occasions for the further explanation or development of the content of my own view. Since this has been part of the purpose, I have chosen only the strongest formulations of views alternative to my own. I am acutely aware of the debt that I owe to those I discuss, both for forcing upon my attention difficulties that demanded that I develop and articulate my thinking and for providing formulations so luminous that I could make my own view clear so to speak by reflection.

I should also add that each view I have considered represents a position on the dialectical landscape the surveying of which is ultimately unavoidable. The necessity of confronting a particular view may not always be obvious at first, but I am confident that it will become so in the end.

Returning to matters of content, we can find another way of looking at the material of this book. At some point in the course of growing up, children learn that "people are animals too." Thereafter it becomes possible to wonder what distinguishes people from other animals. Egocentricity alone, without any thought of claims about the non-physical, might lead one to identify the ability to think, the ability to speak, self-consciousness, and so on as "higher" aspects of people. One can then ask how the "higher" side of people is related to what they plainly share with other animals. Many of the things I have said in this book are parts of the answer to this question.

The specific form that my answer to this question takes is largely determined by the fact that I give a dualistic account of sensations but a physicalistic account of intentionality. This raises the question how sensations fit in with the rest of a person so as to make one integrated whole. This question is as complicated as the object to which it refers. Part of the answer to it is in Chapter I, where I discuss knowledge of sensations. Another part is in Chapter II, where I consider some issues about givenness and conceptual schemes. Still another part comes in the section on inner speech in Chapter III. Chapter V is an important and extended part of the answer. Finally, at the end of Chapter VI, the way in which sensations are related to our ethics becomes clear. Concern with welding together a vision of whole people was often an important factor in determining what problems to take up at what stage of the argument.

In the course of working on this book I have been repeatedly drawn to a careful consideration of the causal complexity that underlies the capacities and abilities that we take for granted. I have found it essential to be clear about the outline of our causal situation and about which questions are causal and which are not. I have also found our causal basis to be a frequent object of wonder and I hope I have been able to convey this sense to my readers.

ACKNOWLEDGMENTS

I would like to express my gratitude to my teachers, and especially to professors Alan Donagan, Reinhardt Grossmann, and Henry Veatch, for their attempts to instill some sense in me; to my colleagues for their willingness to respond to half-baked versions of several of the views in this book; to Edna Wiser and Bernice Powers for their unfailing patience; and to Maureen Ogle for her encouragement.

A portion of Chapter IV appeared in *Southwest Philosophical Studies* 9 (Winter 1983):23–29 under the title "Dretske's Etiological View". Part of the work on this book was done during a Faculty Improvement Leave from Iowa State University in the fall of 1983.

CONTENTS

BRAINS AND PEOPLE

CHAPTER I

Sensations

What Sensations Are

Some Examples

The paradigm examples of sensations, to which I shall refer frequently throughout this chapter, are pains, itches, afterimages, aftertastes, and ringings in the ears. Some things are very like these paradigms but are not denoted by convenient, unambiguous, standard terms. However, since we ought to include things that are very much alike under the same terms, I shall include these things under the term "sensation". Some examples follow.

An afterimage is produced by a bright illumination of the retina, followed by relative darkness. One way of producing the relative darkness is by shutting one's eyes. In this case, one will have an expanse of some color and some shape without any sense of distance. Another way of producing the relative darkness is to look at the wall of a room after looking out of a window during daylight. In this case, one's afterimage, besides having color and shape, appears to be at the same distance as the wall (in general, it appears at the distance at which one's eyes are focused). Having an afterimage in such circumstances is very like noticing something on the wall. For example, if a shiny object has reflected the sun into your eyes and you look at a white wall, you will have a bluish afterimage. Apart from the fact that afterimages tend to "travel", having such an afterimage could be very like noticing a bluish patch (for example, a scuff mark) on the wall. I remember a case of this kind that occurred once when I was deep in thought and staring out a window that had a venetian blind. As I changed position, my eyes fell upon the solid brown trousers I was wearing. I "noticed" some subtle russet lines in the fabric. For a moment I believed I had actually discovered something about the material of my trousers; then I wondered whether I was only having an afterimage. It took me several seconds to become quite sure that the latter was the case.

On another occasion I was standing in the doorway of a colleague's office, leaning against the jamb. A noise began that I thought was either a ringing in my ears or a very loud whistle at some distance from the building I was in. I turned my head to see if that would change the sound. The result was to prove both hypotheses wrong; the noise turned out to be a very faint whistle in a thermostat mounted on the wall about six inches from my ear. This noticing of the faint whistle was as much like having the sensation of ringing in the ears as my afterimage was like noticing russet lines. On the strength of such similarities, I shall take noticing the colors or sounds of things as cases of having sensations.

In this discussion I have not made use of the rubric "notice *that* . . . ." This fact requires some explanation. "Notice" in all of its uses carries the suggestion of coming before our attention for the first time. One kind of thing that can come before our attention is states of affairs. These need not have much to do with the senses. Thus, one can notice that prices have gone up or that there is a similarity between two systems of logic. The "notice *that* . . ."rubric is natural in cases of this kind. (One can, however, forego this rubric in these cases: for example, one can say that one has noticed a price increase or that one has noticed a similarity between two systems of logic.) But sometimes what comes before our attention for the first time is the color of the sunset or a bluish patch or some russet lines or a thin whistle-like sound. These cases are not naturally reported on with the "notice *that* . . ." rubric. Unlike noticings of states of affairs, these noticings have a definite, sensory character.[1]

Parallel remarks can be constructed for noticings of tastes, smells, textures, and temperatures. I shall also count these as sensations, on the strength of the basic argument, that things that in themselves are just like the paradigms of sensations ought to be called "sensations". The same argument leads to including among sensations "seeing stars", the intense visual phenomena occasionally produced by orgasm and of course the pleasurable sensations that go with sexual activity. To be quite general, one has a sensation if one has any item on the list of paradigms or if one has anything that is like these in the way that the examples I have just been giving are like them.

Sensations as Individuals

Sensations are individual things that occur at particular times and that have definite qualities.[2] For example, a pain typically begins shortly after the time when a part of one's body is injured. It may be intense or mild, throbbing or steady. An afterimage occurs shortly after an intense illumination has ceased, begins to fade almost immediately, and gradually disappears. It has a color and a shape. Ringings in the ears have a pitch and a timbre; aftertastes may be sweet or bitter.

1. Noticings are discussed in fuller detail in Chapter V.

2. Someone will say, "Events occur, not things." My reply is that when we are talking about short-lived things, "This thing occurred at t" is a useful ellipsis for "This thing came into existence at t and lasted until a short time later", or "The event that was the onset of existence of this thing occurred at t." For example, "A Pa^{234} (protactinium) atom occurred at t" would be clearly understood to have the sense of "A Pa^{234} atom began to exist at t." (The half-life of a Pa^{234} atom is 1.2 minutes.)

These descriptions of sensations are perfectly literal. "My head began to throb at five o'clock" is as straightforward a remark as "It began to rain at five o'clock" and we are not guilty of mixing metaphors if we say that my head began to throb at the same time that it began to rain. An afterimage can be matched for color with ordinary pain samples. This cannot be done with things that are only metaphorically colored. For example, I can be blue because my love is not returned, but hardly this shade of blue rather than that one, or the same color as a pair of jeans. Similarly, a ringing in my ears is definitely more like the sound of a flute than the sound of a bass fiddle. If I had perfect pitch I could tell you what note it is; and in any case, I can sing the same pitch.

It may seem that the content of the last two paragraphs is too obvious to be worth saying. Certainly denials like "There aren't any intense pains" or "There aren't any yellow afterimages" seem to be so absurd that no one could seriously assert them. Yet there are many philosophers who would find what I have been saying to be false or at least quite misleading. I shall shortly discuss some of the views that lead to such criticism. First, however, I need to make a preliminary comment about the limitations of this discussion.

The key claim that will be under attack is the claim that sensations are individual things. While there are several reasons offered against this claim, there is one very general motivation: it is believed that if we accept the claim we must sooner or later be led to some grievously wrong or absurd theory. It would be unprofitable to try to respond to this motivation *here,* that is, in the immediately following discussion. The only proper response would be to start with the claim that is in contention and show how it can be developed in a fruitful and coherent way. I believe that the present chapter, Chapter II, and parts of Chapter V go a long way toward carrying out exactly this task. In the immediately following discussion, however, all I can do, and all I should be expected to do, is to say why I am not, at the beginning, dissuaded from beginning as I have. I shall do this by considering alternative suggestions and showing either that they have severe problems of their own or that, taken as criticisms of my claim about sensations, they are inconclusive.

The first criticism I shall consider concerns my claim that sensations are literally colored, shaped, pitched, and so on. The argument is that things that are, say, literally round can be rolled. Since sensations cannot be rolled, one might conclude that sensations cannot be literally round. Again, it may be premised that what is literally yellow must preferentially reflect light of a certain wavelength. Since sensations reflect no light one might conclude that they cannot be literally yellow.

The first premises of these arguments are, however, false. Globs of jello and frosty haloes around the moon can clearly be literally round, but they cannot be rolled. Parts of rainbows are plainly literally yellow, but we will find no band of water droplets in the sky that preferentially reflects light of a certain wavelength. Rollability and preferential reflectivity follow not from roundness and yellowness alone, but only from these combined with further properties like rigidity and three dimensionality. Typical yellow things may have preferential reflectivity, but the fact that sensations lack this property shows only that they are atypical yellow things, not that they are not literally yellow.

The general point that I draw from these examples is that atypicality of sensations is not a good reason to deny the literalness of their classification under such terms as "yellow", "round", "F♯", "reedy", "bitter", and so on. These classifications are not pieces of philosophical legislation; they are the way ordinary people describe their sensations. I am not, of course, committed to the view that there could never be reason to give up an ordinary way of speaking. I do say that we have not yet been provided with a good argument for giving up the literal yellowness and so on of sensations and that, in the absence of such an argument, it would be unreasonable to begin on any assumption other than that sensations are literally colored, shaped, pitched, and so on.

The next criticism I shall take up focuses not so much on the qualities of sensations as the status of what *has* these qualities. This criticism arises from the view known as "adverbialism".[3] According to this view, "Jones has a pain" and similar constructions have a misleading grammatical form that suggests to us that there is such a thing as *a pain*. In reality, it would be better to focus our attention on "Jones hurts." This does not represent Jones as "having" a *thing*. It represents Jones as being in a certain condition or *state*. It is not so easy to find convenient ways for expressing the point of this view for cases like afterimages, but we can always make up appropriate state-ascribing phrases. We can say, for example, that Jones is in a yellow oval afterimaging state, that Jones afterimages yellow ovally, or that Jones senses yellow ovally. The point of all these locutions is to bring our description of certain happenings into surface conformity with the philosophical claim that what I have called "having sensations" is—is *really*—being in some state.

We have to add something to this view and it is important to understand why. The problem is that, once we open ourselves to contrived locutions, anything at all can be phrased as a state. A finger is as "thingish" a thing as one could wish for. If I'd been born with six of them on each hand, I would certainly have two extra fingers. But I can rephrase this into state terminology by talking about being in a two-extra-fingered state. Likewise, if I have staphylococcus bacteria in my body I can be described as being in a

3. The classical source for this view is Roderick Chisholm, *Perceiving: A Philosophical Study* (Ithaca, N.Y.: Cornell University Press, 1957). Wilfrid Sellars is often thought of as an adverbialist. He does indeed offer an adverbial account *at one level*. For Sellars, however, this level is not ultimate. Thus, Sellars does not count as an adverbialist in the sense intended here. See my "Sellarsian Materialism", *Philosophy of Science* 49 (1982); 212–227 and later sections of this chapter.

staphylococcus-infested state, or as suffering staphylococcus-in-festedly. In the absence of some addition to adverbialism, it is too weak to be an *alternative* to any view, since it incorporates them all.

It should be obvious what addition is needed. We must under-stand adverbialism to hold that when people hurt, sense yellow ovally, sense ringingly, and so on they are in states that cannot be analyzed as involving individual things that have the properties ad-verbially attributed to those states. That is, hurting does not involve *a pain,* where this is conceived of as an individual thing of a certain kind; what happens after a bright blue illumination does not involve an individual thing that is yellow, and so on.

This strengthened view, however, encounters the following diffi-culty. Whatever language we use, a full description of our sensory goings on will have to convey the fact that color is *somehow* in-volved in afterimaging, that pitch is *somehow* involved in ringings in the ears, and so on. But we have no understanding of how yellow, for example, or C♯ could come into such states except as properties of individuals. We do not know what a *yellow state* is—unless we mean a yellow state *of something,* that is, something's being yellow. Thus, we could say of a dandelion that it was in its yellow state, meaning that it had begun to bloom and had not yet turned to seed. But understanding this is parasitic upon attributing yellow to the bloom, which is an individual thing. Adverbialists refuse any ana-logue to this explanation for afterimaging. On their account, when Jones afterimages yellow ovally, nothing that has any special rela-tion to Jones is a yellow oval. The difficulty in this view is that it does not provide any account of how colors, shapes, pitches, and so on can come into sensations even though, clearly, they do come into sensations in some way.

There is, however, a view that can be added to adverbialism in order to provide what I have just said is lacking. This view is called "topic neutralism" and I shall shortly state and evaluate it. Before doing so, however, I wish to comment on another view that is in some ways similar to adverbialism even though the basic inspiration comes from a different source. This view originated with G. E. M. Anscombe and her formulation remains the clearest for our purposes.[4] The main point of interest here is that Anscombe thinks that many people have been led to introduce Berkeleyan ideas (or Humean impressions, or Russellian sense-data) through a failure to appreciate the logic of verbs of perception. They have, on her account, regarded sentences like "Jones sees a stag" as expressing a relation between Jones and some other entity. They have then noted that there is a sense in which people can be said to see a stag even if what they are seeing is in fact not a stag (or even if there is no ordinary thing at all in front of them). They have then concluded that the entity to which people are related when they see a stag cannot be a stag, but must be some other kind of entity, stag-like in some respects, but guaranteed to be present whether or not there is a stag. In short, they have concluded that seeing (and, of course, perceiving in the other modes) involves standing in a relation to a sense-datum.

Anscombe's way of avoiding this conclusion depends on setting up an analogy with our way of giving the direct object of a sentence. The answer to the question, "What is the direct object of the sentence 'John gave Mary a book'?" is "A book." "A book" as used here does not refer to the words "a book"—for the sentence for whose direct object we are asked does not say that John gave Mary

4. G. E. M. Anscombe, "The Intentionality of Sensation: A Grammatical Feature", In R. J. Butler, ed., *Analytical Philosophy* (2nd ser.; Oxford: Basil Blackwell, 1965). Parenthetical numbers in the following discussion refer to this volume. Anscombe's idea has been taken up by Jaako Hintikka in "On the Logic of Perception" in his *Models for Modalities* (Dordrecht: Reidel, 1969), and after him by Richmond Thomason in "Perception and Individuation" in Milton K. Munitz, ed., *Logic and Ontology* (New York: New York University Press, 1973), and by Robert Kraut in "Sensory States and Sensory Objects," *Nous* 16 (1982): 277–293. The focus of interest of these latter two, however, diverges from our main concerns.

some words. But neither do the words "a book" refer to a book—
for there is no book of which the sentence says that John gave it to
Mary. Anscombe's conclusion is that the words "a book", when
used to give the direct object of a sentence, have a "special use". I
will introduce a term of my own here and call this a "non-referen-
tial" use. We can say, then, that even though we can give the direct
object of a sentence, when we do so we are not giving (referring to)
an *object* (in the sense of some entity). Now, Anscombe's idea is that
when we give the (intentional) object of perceptual verbs we use
words in an analogous, special sense. In saying, for example, that
Jones sees *a stag,* we refer neither to the words "a stag" nor to any
entity that corresponds to those words. If we are not referring to any
entity, then of course we are not referring to a peculiar kind of entity
such as a sense-datum.

I want to make two groups of comments on this account. The first
brings out a similarity that it has to my own view. The second brings
out a similarity that it has to adverbialism and thus will lead us back
to further consideration of that position.

The point of similarity with my own view is the denial of sense-
data. Sense-data are items that are said to be perceived or to be
sensed or to be objects of a relation of awareness. None of these
things have been or will be said of sensations, which are thus not to
be assimilated to sense-data. I will say that sensations are *had* by
people; but the explanation of "having" will emphatically not involve a relation of awareness. This topic requires extended argument, however, which must be deferred until later. Here, at the preliminary stage, I can only put forward as a clarification of the view I
am proposing, that it is not to be confused with sense-datum
theories.

A related point is that I have not based anything I have said on
any claims about perception or perception reports. I have begun
with such things as pains and afterimages and have pointed to certain things that are similar to these. I have not said or implied, nor

do I believe, that sensations are part of the analysis of perception. Once again, we have come to a contentious matter that requires explanation and argument. We shall return to it later,[5] but in the preliminary stage it should nonetheless be clear that I am not proceeding in a way that Anscombe has already examined and shown to be flawed.

The point of similarity between Anscombe's view and adverbialism lies in its implicit recognition of states of people for which some account is needed. To bring this out, consider again "Jones saw a stag." Let us take this in the sense in which it could be true although no stag is present and let us agree that, so taken it does not commit us to a staggish sense-datum. Nonetheless, it tells us *something* about Jones; it tells us something that contrasts in a clearly understandable way with, for example, "Jones saw a bear" (taken in the same way). In taking these sentences in the way intended, we are forced to regard them as characterizing Jones, or perhaps Jones' state of mind or perceptual state.[6] We are entitled to ask what constitutes such states and what differences in what things make the differences among them. Since colors, shapes, pitches, and so on are among the *prima facie* differences among these states, we are entitled to ask just how they enter into them.

Now, there is a way of answering this question that will cover some cases without leading either to sensations or to the problem concerning adverbialism. For, in some cases, we can assimilate dif-

5. See the last section of Chapter V.

6. This point comes out in Hintikka's and Thomason's papers in the use of the phrase "compatible with what a perceiver perceives", where it is clear that the last four words are not simply a way of referring to a physical object that is perceived by a perceiver. See Hintikka, "On the Logic of Perception", p. 155, and Thomason, "Perception and Individuation", p. 262. Kraut, "Sensory States and Sensory Objects", p. 282, is explicit about states and suggests the topic-neutralist view we are about to take up. He says that Macbeth's well-known "experience is a state which *would* typically be induced by dagger irradiation events."

ferences of perception to differences in what is believed.[7] In these cases, colors, shapes, pitches, and so on can enter a state merely as properties that some ordinary thing is believed or not believed to have. However, not all cases can be treated in this way. Anscombe gives an example, citing "H. H. Price's mescaline illusion, when without any derangement of his judgment he was able to describe what he saw—a great pile of leaves on his counterpane, which he knew not to be there" (179). In such cases, visual properties are involved in some way other than as (intentional) objects of believing; and we have returned to the question we asked of adverbialism, namely, what kind of involvement this is.

Anscombe herself allows that in the case of Price's illusion "the words 'a pile of leaves' were intended only as a description of an impression" (179). Many, however, will not find this acceptable and will turn to a topic-neutralist account of the required states. Having arrived at the need for this view from two different directions, we can now begin to examine it.

Topic Neutralism explains what it is to be in a state of a certain kind by the following equivalence.[8]

(TN) Where F is a property and P is a person,
    P is in an F state (or, P senses F-ly)
  if and only if
    P is in a state that is normally brought about by the operation of F physical objects on the appropriate sense organ.

7. For Hintikka and Thomason, the "perceives *that* . . ." rubric is basic.

8. A classical source for this much-used view is J. J. C. Smart, *Philosophy and Scientific Realism* (London: Routledge & Kegan Paul, 1963). Some forms of topic neutralism emphasize what a state causes rather than what causes it. Since there is no behavior characteristic of afterimages, such an emphasis would be inappropriate here.

When adverbialists add (TN) to their view, they may say that when we are afterimaging yellow ovally we are in a brain state that is normally brought about by our seeing yellow ovals. This is taken to explicate the way in which yellow is connected to our sensations. Such an explanation presupposes that we have parts (for example, neurons and synapses) that can be in this or that state; but none of them need be held to be a yellow individual.

While the attraction of topic neutralism is understandable, it does not really do the job required of it. The right side of (TN) is not an adequate account of the left side, provided that the left side is supposed to apply to cases that we ordinarily indicate by such statements as "*P* has a pain" and "*P* has a yellow afterimage." We can see this most directly by considering the following thought experiment. Afterimages have the color that is complimentary to the color of the illumination that causes them. Let us imagine that some people have looked at a bright blue oval light and have then looked at a dark wall in a comparatively ill-lighted room. Now they will have a yellow oval afterimage or, in the adverbialists' language, they will sense yellow ovally. When their afterimages have faded, let them look at the light again and then look away from it at the wall. Then they will sense yellow ovally once again. Now, there are not so very many yellow oval objects; so if these people become fanatical about sensing yellow ovally, they can repeat the above procedure so many times that more of their sensings yellow ovally will have been brought about by blue lights than by yellow physical objects. In such a case, (TN) would lead us to say that they were sensing bluely. However, this is an extremely counterintuitive result; no one, I think, will accept the view that the imagined change of relative frequencies of causes of afterimages must change (as we ordinarily speak) our yellow afterimages into blue ones. Our thought experiment, moreover, makes it pretty clear where the adverbialists' attempt to use (TN) has gone wrong. When we describe our sensations, we describe what they *are* and not merely what they are (causally) related to. The use of (TN) provides only a relational characterization and thus brings us no closer to having a new way of understanding what those things are that occur, for example, after illumination by bright blue lights.

Someone may be tempted to object that my criticism of the use of (TN) is unsuccessful because it appeals merely to possible worlds, whereas in the actual world (TN) is true. The observation that prompts this objection is correct, but it is irrelevant. The question is not whether (TN) is true, that is, with its "if and only if" taken materially, but whether it is an equivalence that explains the sense in which what happens after bright blue illuminations involves yellow. Such an explanation would have to apply to possible as well as actual cases.

Again, someone may object that we have omitted an important normalcy condition. According to this objection, the right side of (TN) should have read, "P is in a state that is normally brought about by the operation of F physical objects on the appropriate sense organs *in the normal manner for those organs*." Now, if "normal" here means "usual" we can reinstate our criticism by conducting our thought experiment in a somewhat more bizarre possible world. In this world, there are many bright light sources floating about and, as a result, people have more afterimages than non-afterimage seeings. So their sensings yellowly would be more often than not caused by blue physical objects. That, at least, is the plausible way to describe the situation. The amended (TN) would, however, require us to say—again, most counterintuitively—that the afterimages caused by exposure to blue lights (and other sensings like them) would be sensings bluely.

In response to this point, defenders of (TN) may suggest that the additional clause "in the normal manner for those organs" can be read in a way that does not give rise to the counterintuitive result just obtained. There are, in fact, two alternative ways in which that clause may be read. One of these takes "normal" to mean what is normal in the *actual* world, not in whatever possible world we happen to be considering. The other takes "normal manner" to mean "manner of operation (of sense organs) that usually results in things seeming to be as they really are." The first of these readings is, however, unsuccessful for what should be a familiar reason: (TN) is not meant to be merely an extensional equivalence, but an explanation of what it means to say that sensings are, for example, yellow. This makes the restriction to the actual world arbitrary. The arbitrariness here might be hidden, however, if one also accepts the second reading. That is, one might think that attention to the normal manner of operation of sense organs in the actual world is not arbitrary *because* this is the manner in which things usually seem to be as they really are. This latter point, however, is *not* one that adverbialists can use. For, if they appeal to it, they legitimately may be asked to give an account of seeming; this, according to their view, involves sensing *F*-ly or being in an *F* state, and these are just what (TN) was supposed to have helped to explicate. Thus, appeal to this last reading of "in the normal manner for those organs" would throw adverbialists into a circularity in which seeming would be explained, eventually, by seeming.

Before leaving adverbialism we must give brief consideration to an attempt to explicate "sensing *F*-ly" that is quite different from anything so far mentioned. We can say without philosophical puzzlement that there was a dull glow in the northern sky. This might be taken to support the view that there can be a glowing dully, or that the sky can be in a dully glowing state, without there being any individual thing that glows dully. Such cases, however, will not serve the adverbialists' purpose. I indicated in footnote 2 that event talk finds an easy purchase in discussions of ephemeral individuals. This is sometimes true of state talk also. Thus, in the case described we might just as well have said that there was a patch of a certain shape that emitted a small amount of light, that began to exist at a certain time and place in the sky, and that lasted for just so long. Adverbialists, however, need a way of classifying states into kinds that is plainly distinct from the classification of kinds of individuals, whether ephemeral or enduring.[9]

Adverbialism may be described as an attempt to *recategorize*[10] sensations, that is, to categorize them as states rather than individuals. The view to which I now turn proposes rather to *eliminate* them. I will discuss this proposal in connection with the work of D. C. Dennett. Dennett does not deny that there are true sentences of the form "Jones has a pain" or "Jones has a yellow afterimage." He does, however, deny that one is entitled to move from these to "There is a pain that Jones has" or "There is a yellow afterimage that Jones has" at least if these are construed as serious claims to the effect that an individual thing of some definite kind exists. His view is that to make such a transition would be like moving from truths like "John acted for Tom's sake" and "Bob strained his voice" to "There is a sake of Tom's for which John acted" and "There is a voice such that Bob strained it."[11] These are indeed absurd moves; but why are the moves to the existence of pains and afterimages supposed to be similar? In one suggestive passage, Dennett says:

> Could any sense be made of the supposition that a person might hit his thumb with a hammer and be suddenly and over-whelmingly compelled to drop the hammer, suck the thumb, dance about, shriek, moan, cry, etc., and yet *still* not be experiencing pain? That is, one would not be acting in this case, as on

9. Michael Levin defends a form of adverbialism in his book, *Metaphysics and the Mind-Body Problem* (Oxford: Oxford University Press, 1979). However, since his view raises issues that concern the problem of the self, I will not explain why his defense is unsuccessful until Chapter V.

10. Wilfrid Sellars has used this term in the present sense. See the third of his Carus Lectures, "Is Consciousness Physical?" secs. 36–49, in *The Monist* 64 (1981): 72–74.

11. See D. C. Dennett, *Content and Consciousness* (New York: Humanities Press, 1969), chap. 1 and pp. 90–96.

a stage; one would be compelled. One would be physically incapable of responding to polite applause with a smiling bow.
Positing some horrible (but otherwise indescribable) quality or
phenomenon to accompany such a compelled performance is
entirely gratuitous.[12]

This and the surrounding text suggest the following argument. We
base our attributions of sensations on people's behavior. People who
have the disposition to produce behavior of the kind that would
support our attributing pain to them, and to do so indefinitely and
in all circumstances, are correctly said to be in pain. In analyzing
such cases we are entitled to claim the existence only of people, their
behavior, and anything we need to explain their behavior. Pains,
however, do not explain behavior. Thus, we are not entitled to the
existence of pains as individual things. There are two reasons for
saying that pains do not explain behavior. First, what does explain
behavior is the firing of sensory neurons, followed by firings of neurons in the spinal cord and brain, followed by firings of motor neurons. Second, if attributing pain is regarded as attributing, for example, a disposition to groan, trying to explain groans by pains
would come to no more than saying that people groan because they
are disposed to groan.

This argument raises some issues that we cannot address until
later. However, we can say enough to show why it would be unreasonable to begin by accepting it. First, the supposition in the first
sentence of the quotation from *Content and Consciousness* is perfectly intelligible. We know that some "pain behavior" occurs prior
to any painful sensation. This is clearest in cases like putting one's
hand on a hot iron, where one withdraws the hand and immediately
afterward begins to feel the pain.[13] We know that there are involun-

12. *Ibid.*, pp. 94–95.
13. This claim is not idiosyncratic. See Bede Rundle, *Perception, Sensation and
Verification* (Oxford: Oxford University Press, 1972), p. 126.

tary muscle spasms. We can imagine some Martians doing a bit of neural bypassing work on us, in which they block connections from afferent neurons to pain centers but connect those afferents to efferents by new paths, with the result that our muscle contractions are just what they would have been without the interference. This *may* be causally impossible; we do not, however, know that it is. A story that imagined such Martians would not be conceptually flawed in the way that a story would be if it said that there were not adding machines in its world, but that there were machines that printed out correct sums when you punched pairs of buttons with numbers on them.

Behaviorism finds some plausibility in cases where there is an easily discernible characteristic behavior. However, if behaviorism were the right way to look at pains, it ought to be right for other sensations. Let us try it out with afterimages. We would have to say that people sometimes found themselves impelled to say "My afterimage was yellow just now" or "My afterimage was blue just now." Since there is no non-verbal behavior that is characteristic of those who have yellow or blue afterimages, we would have to suppose that there is nothing more to the truth of the above claims than that competent speakers are impelled to say them.[14] We would have to say that there is nothing blue or yellow entering into these situations, but at most the words "blue" and "yellow" and brain states normally brought about by blue or yellow things. All these consequences are absurd on their face. It would therefore be unreasonable to accept the view that leads to them unless all alternatives proved to have defects at least as grave.

Our recent discussion began with a quotation of Dennett's that has a strongly behaviorist ring. Some may object that, after all, Dennett is a functionalist (in some senses of this much-used term) and

---

14. Bede Rundle is willing to accept this consequence of behaviorism (or, more generally, verificationism). See *ibid.*, pp. 137–145.

that we should really be considering a functionalist attempt to avoid beginning with sensations as individual things. Others may notice that I have been offering a version of what has become known as an "absent qualia" argument and may wish for a more explicit formulation of this argument. The following discussion is designed to satisfy both demands.[15]

To bring out what functionalism adds to behaviorism I will recast my discussion of behaviorism in the following way. First, we may represent behaviorism as requiring us to focus our attention on the inputs to and outputs from an organism. According to behaviorism, an organism has a pain if and only if it exhibits certain pairings of input-output sequences. Now, my argument was, in effect, that pains have internal causes, that is, neuron firings in various paths in our bodies. These paths may begin anywhere in our bodies and they end in the proximate causes of pains, namely, neuron firings in our brains. The evidence for this is straightforward and is well know to anesthesiologists and pain researchers. Since effects that are only undetectably different can be produced by quite different causes it is always possible in principle to produce a sequence of input-output pairings that would be just like those of a person with a pain even though the internal, neural paths utilized were quite different from the usual ones and did not result in the activation of the neurons that are the proximate causes of pains. For this reason, we ought not to agree that an organism's exhibiting certain input-output pairings is just all there is to the fact that it has a pain.

15. See, e.g., Ned Block, "Troubles with Functionalism", in C. Wade Savage, ed., *Perception and Cognition: Issues in the Foundations of Psychology, Minnesota Studies in the Philosophy of Science,* vol. 9 (Minneapolis: University of Minnesota Press, 1978), pp. 261–325; Sydney Shoemaker, "Functionalism and Qualia", *Philosophical Studies* 27 (1975): 291–315; Block's reply, "Are Absent Qualia Impossible?" *Philosophical Review* 89 (1980): 257–274, and A. D. Kline and W. S. Robinson, "On *Brainstorms*", *Nature and System* 2 (1980); 37–48.

Behaviorism, and my criticism of it, can be given a formulation in functionalistic terms. To see how, let us consider one of the basic ideas of functionalism. We can formulate it as the Functionalist Principle:

(FP) For an organism to be the subject of a mental predicate M is for that organism to perform the function F.

The idea encapsulated in this principle is commonly illustrated by examples like the following. For a thing to be a valve-lifter (a subject of the predicate "valve-lifter") is for that thing to perform the function of lifting valves. A little less trivially, for a thing to be a heart is for it to perform the function of pumping blood. Now, if you fill out this pattern by taking "has a pain" for "M" and "exhibiting one of a certain set of sequences of input-output pairings" for "F" you get a way of stating behaviorism. You can express the idea in abbreviated form by saying that to have a pain is to perform a certain function. The criticism I have raised can then also be put shortly: You can, in principle, get the function performed without involving those neurons that are the proximate causes of pains, and thus without getting the organism to have pains.

The advantage that functionalism has over behaviorism is that it can offer alternative substituends for "F" in (FP). This is, in effect, what Dennett does in his paper "Why You Can't Make a Computer That Feels Pain."[16] Dennett is motivated by some considerations that emerge when you take a close look at what is known of the physiology of (the causes of) pain and at the different effects that are brought about by different anesthetics and different times of admin-

---

16. This paper is reprinted in Dennett, *Brainstorms* (Bradford Books, 1978), pp. 190–229. Dennett worries that there is no fully consistent specification of the function whose satisfaction by an organism would amount to its having a pain—because our concept of pain may have contradictory elements. I shall, however, abstract from this worry in order to bring out the main flaw in the functionalist treatment of pain.

istration. This evidence leads naturally to the postulation of certain internal structures each of which performs some function and has certain relations to the other structures. Now, since these internal structures are known in the first place by what functions they perform,[17] it is natural to include them in the specification of what an organism must do in order to be properly said to be having a pain. That is, one may choose for "*F*" in (FP) the function "exhibiting one of a certain set of sequences of input-output pairings by means of internal causes whose parts perform certain functions and stand in certain relations."

Despite the added complexity of this view, the criticism of it is exactly the same as the one made against behaviorism. To bring this out it will be helpful to remind ourselves that functions can, in general, be performed by different structures.[18] Thus, for example, we can have different designs for valve-lifters and hearts may be two- or four-chambered. This fact ensures that it will always be logically possible to get the function specified at the end of the last paragraph performed without involving neural patterns that are causes of pains. It will therefore be possible to get that function performed without producing pains. Thus an organism's performing that function is not the same thing as its being in pain.

Functionalists may be inclined to object here that I am begging the question against them by assuming that pains have neural causes and thus are (ephemeral) individuals. However, it is not I who introduce an assumption that conflicts with functionalism. Talk about the neural causes of pain is very straightforward talk engaged in by medical researchers and neurophysiologists.[19] Of course, if we cannot make sense of a view that embraces sensations as individuals,

17. I say "in the first place" because functionalists envisage eventual neurophysiological discovery of the groups of neurons that actually perform the various functions in us.

18. For elaboration of the function-structure relation see W. S. Robinson and A. D. Kline, "Dennett's Dilemma", *Journal of Critical Analysis* 8 (1979): 1–4.

19. Richard Schlagel has collected a number of statements by neurophysiologists

we might have to consider giving up this way of talking (and think-ing). But it would not be reasonable to give it up for any other rea-son; and it would surely not be reasonable to *begin* the discussion of sensations by assuming that this way of talking is misguided.

The way in which I have presented behaviorism and func-tionalism suggests a further development. Dennett's proposal al-ready relied on some medical research. Let us imagine that we have a great deal more at hand. We may suppose that we have investigat-ed the differential effects of drugs, lesions, and electrode stimula-tion. We may imagine that we have evidence for a complete story about which neuron firings cause which pains. Now, whatever evi-dence of this kind we may have may be phrased in the language of functionalism. For example, where we might ordinarily say "This neuron is implicated in causation of pain because freezing it stops the patient's pain" a philosopher could say "When the patient has a pain, there must be a structure that performs the function of stop-ping the pain behavior when frozen." If we make this sort of move repeatedly, we can turn *all* our evidence concerning the causation of pain into a very complex function. We can briefly describe it as:

(E)　the function of working in such a way as to produce
　　　each item of evidence that we have regarding (as we
　　　ordinarily say) the causes of pains.

The point of this move is that it would no longer be possible to have any reason to deny that a subject had a pain once it was established that the function (E) was being performed. However, this move holds little comfort for functionalists. The reason is that it com-pletely trivializes the notion of performing a function. To see this, consider an alternative description:

(C)　the function of working in such a way as to cause pains.

---

that indicate that they think of sensations as caused by neural firings, but as lying beyond the bounds of the physiological. See his "The Mind-Brain Identity Impasse", *American Philosophical Quarterly* 14 (1977): esp. 231–237.

(E) could be thought to be significantly different from (C) only if one were to assume that what is ordinarily called "evidence about the causes of pains" cannot really be good evidence for genuine causes. This, however, is an implausible assumption that neural scientists would not make. This leaves functionalism with the following dilemma: Either it specifies the function required for having pains as in (E), in which case it has no reasoned way of denying that pains are individual things (no reasoned way of distinguishing the performance of (E) from the performance of (C)); or it specifies the function in some other way, in which case it fails because it will be logically possible to satisfy the function without producing pains.

We have now examined the most plausible of the views that recommend against taking sensations to be individuals. None of them has proved reasonable, at least as a starting point. We are thus justified in taking sensations to be individuals and proceeding to raise further questions about them.

Dualism

Against Identity

My friend Susan and the person who robbed the bank, whoever it may be, are individual things. Whether it is polite or not, it certainly makes sense to ask whether Susan is the person who robbed the bank. Equivalently, we can ask whether Susan is identical with the person who robbed the bank, or whether Susan and the robber are two individual things or only one. It is a general fact about individual things that such questions always make sense, even if the answer may be very obviously "No."

Since sensations are individual things it makes sense to ask whether they are identical with any things that we know about from a different perspective. If there are such items, they must at least be the sort of thing that exists when, and only when, sensations exist. There is only one class of individuals for which it is plausible that this condition holds, namely, groups of neurons that are firing in a certain order and frequency. This way of describing such individuals, however, requires some explanation.

Most writers have spoken of brain *states* as the candidates for identification with sensations. However, we have just argued for treating sensations as individuals and thus whatever we say a sensation might be identical with had better be an individual too. Now, we cannot take a part of a brain to be a sensation, since we have our brain cells for a relatively long time, while sensations come and go. To find an individual that could even be a candidate for identification with a sensation we must take a brain part (that is, a group of cells, presumably neural cells, that is, neurons) just while it is in a certain state of agitation. This may be easier to grasp if we consider the analogous case of lightning. Lightning is said to be (identical with) electrical discharge. A particular flash of lightning—which is an ephemeral individual—is thus identical with a particular electrical discharge. An electrical discharge, however, cannot be identified with the electrons that compose it, for they exist long after the discharge is over. We must rather identify the electrical discharge with the electrons that compose it, *while they are flowing.*

There are many philosophers who believe, in effect, that sensations are identical with groups of firing neurons.[20] Among the rea-

---

20. I say "in effect" because the ontology of ephemeral individuals is not a common presupposition. When adjustment is made for difference of ontology (which raises no substantive issue here) one obtains the identity claim that I will be discussing. For representative proponents of the identity view for sensations see J. J. C. Smart, "Sensations and Brain Processes", *Philosophical Review* 68 (1959): 141–156; D. M. Armstrong, *A Materialist Theory of the Mind* (London: Routledge & Kegan Paul, 1968); Donald Davidson, "Mental Events", in Lawrence Foster and J. W. Swanson, eds., *Experience and Theory* (Amherst: University of Massachusetts Press, 1970); and Levin, *Metaphysics and the Mind-Body Problem.*

sons for this view is the fact that if sensations are not thus identical, then it is difficult to see how they can be physical at all. It is, however, plausible to think that there is nothing other than sensations that is not physical. Thus, if sensations are not identical with groups of firing neurons they would be the only exception to the physicality of the universe. This is often thought to be inelegant, unscientific, and in violation of the principle that our best theories ought to be simple and very general.[21]

My own view is that sensations are *caused by* but not *identical with* groups of firing neurons.[22] I hold that, for example, when we are burned, neurons whose ends are in the skin are caused to fire repeatedly. These firings cause other neurons to fire, some of which may initiate reflex actions, but some of which (perhaps after several intermediate neurons have fired) produce the firing of a group of neurons in my brain. This condition obtaining in this group of neurons produces a pain with a certain intensity and locational quality. Similarly, when my retina is illuminated, rods and cones are stimulated. This stimulus produces firings in neurons in the optic nerve and subsequently in other neurons. There is at least one part of my brain (and probably several) such that whenever it gets into a certain condition I have a yellow afterimage. It seems likely that if that part gets into a similar, but not exactly similar, condition or if a similar part of my brain gets into a similar condition, I will have an orange afterimage instead. A parallel story holds for aftertastes and

21. This argument occurs in J. J. C. Smart, "Sensations and Brain Processes". See also Dennett, *Content and Consciousness*, pp. 4–5.

22. Some will say, "Only *events* can be causes and effects." These will have to translate my rubric "(ephemeral individual) *A* causes (ephemeral individual) *B*" into "the coming into existence of *A* causes the coming into existence of *B* and the existing of *A* at *t* causes the existing of *B* at $t + dt$." Others will say, "Only *facts* can be causes and effects." These must translate my rubric into "the fact that *A* exists at *t* causes the fact that *B* exists at $t + dt$." No substantive argument in the present context is affected by choice among these idioms.

ringings in the ears. Finally, it seems plausible to suppose that the similarity holding between afterimages and noticing the colors of things is paralleled by a similarity of causes. If this is right, then, for example, when we notice the yellow color of something we come to have some group of neurons firing in a certain way; and such a pattern of firing in this group of neurons could be produced on another occasion by bright blue illumination followed by relative darkness.

I shall not argue for the causal details of this account. They are not in conflict with available physiological evidence and they are the most plausible explanation of obvious facts. The details are not in contention between my view and that of identity theorists. The only issue between us is whether I am right in supposing that certain groups of firing neurons are causes of sensations or whether they are right in supposing that those same ephemeral individuals are identical with sensations. I shall now proceed to an argument designed to confront this issue directly and settle it.

In arguing against the identity view I shall make use of the following Reducibility Principle:

(RP)   If an object is in a strict sense a system of objects, then every property of the object must be explainable by reference to the fact that its constituents have such and such qualities and stand in such and such relations.[23]

Let us have some examples of the application of this principle. A ladder, we say, is nothing but rungs and slats in a certain arrangement. According to the reducibility principle, its properties, for example, being useful for getting onto a roof, ought to be explainable by reference to the properties and arrangement of its parts. This is the case. Once we understand how the rungs fit into the slats and

23. This is a variant of a principle enunciated by Wilfrid Sellars. See his *Science, Perception and Reality* (London: Routledge & Kegan Paul, 1963), p. 27.

that both are rigid, we understand why stepping on a rung, when the ladder is in a certain position, gets you nearer the roof. A less homely example is this one: Bodies of water are nothing but collections of H_2O molecules. According to the reducibility principle we ought to be able to explain the properties of bodies of water—for example, transparency or utility as a solvent—by reference to what physics and chemistry tell us about H_2O molecules. There is nothing trivial about doing this, but we do believe it can be done and we have long stories to tell about how molecular resonance affects absorption of light and how H_2O molecules cluster around molecules of dissolved compounds.[24]

We ought to accept the reducibility principle because without it identity claims would become uninteresting, trivial, and useless for their intended purpose. It is only because we think the properties of water can be explained by the properties and arrangements of H_2O molecules that we think the claim "bodies of water are nothing but collections of H_2O molecules" is interesting or helpful in unifying our thoughts about water and our reflections on chemistry. To see the point of this remark, try imagining that, after telling our complete physical and chemical story about H_2O molecules, we have no idea why it should turn out that collections of them should pass light or dissolve salt. In such a case it would probably still not be easy to derive a contradiction from the identity claim. But there could be no good reason to accept it. It would falsely suggest that our science applied to water whereas in fact it would leave everything we always wanted to know about water—why it is transparent, a good solvent, and so on—outside of its account.

This situation, which is merely imaginary in the case of water and physics and chemistry, is what actually obtains in the case of sensa-

---

24. For a discussion of absorption see the relevant sections of R. W. Ditchburn, *Light* (New York: Interscience, 1953). For the mechanism of dissolving see Garth L. Lee and Harris O. Van Orden, *General Chemistry* (Philadelphia: W. B. Saunders, 1960), pp. 213–214.

tions and neurophysiology. This becomes obvious the moment you articulate particular cases. Consider a pain. If the identity view is true then it is composed of neurons firing in a certain way. The qualities and relations assigned to neurons by neurophysiology are all of kinds similar to these: spatial relations, order of firing, frequency of firing, energy expended in a firing, time between firings, ratios among some of the foregoing, and amount of electrical potential produced by a firing at a synapse. It is part of my own view that there is some set of such properties and relations that will always cause me to have a pain when it is instantiated by some group of neurons. What I am denying is that such a group of neurons could *compose* a pain. There is no story that we can so much as imagine that talks about the order, frequency, intensity, and so on of neural firings but ends with our seeing why *such* a collection of neurons has to be a pain. We can *see why* a certain arrangement of rigid wood pieces has to do what we expect ladders to do. After examining a mechanical adding machine we can *see why,* in virtue of the cogs and levers being rigid and arranged in the way they are, the machine should give right answers to addition problems. We can come to *see why* a plant is phototropic from knowing about its structure and the way in which light affects the production of growth hormone.[25] Nothing like this happens with sensations and neural properties. There is no understanding of why a pain should require firing frequency ratios of, say, $2 : 1 : 5 : 3$ rather than $3 : 2 : 5 : 4$. There is no seeing why one of these has to be part of a pain while the other could only be a constituent of an itch. There is no seeing why an intensity ratio of $8 : 6 : 7 : 3$ should form yellow in an afterimage rather than orange.

This absence of a certain kind of understanding is not merely a temporary limitation. There are plenty of cases in which we don't know how a thing does what it does but where we can think up plausible stories that we might someday be able to test. With sensa-

25. See Victor A. Greulach, "Plant Movements", *Scientific American* 192 (1955): 102.

tions, however, we don't even have a model of what it would be like to "find out" how intensities or firing orders make up the painful or yellow or C♯ character of a sensation.

Many of those who have heard the argument I have just presented have been inclined to make an objection at this point. The objection is that we could, after all, have evidence for the identity of sensations and groups of firing neurons by discovering that every time a certain kind of the latter occurred so did a certain kind of sensation. Of course, *if* the identity view were correct, then such co-occurrences would have to be found. However, one cannot reason from co-occurrences to identity, because co-occurrences are equally to be expected on the assumption that groups of firing neurons cause sensations. Even if one recognizes this, one may be inclined to think that at any rate the identity view would be one hypothesis that could explain observed co-occurrences of the kind described above. This inclination must be resisted, however, since it is unreasonable to introduce hypotheses that we do not fully understand; and as I have just been arguing, we do not fully understand what it would be for sensations to be identical with groups of firing neurons.

Another frequent objection at this point rests on a species of topic neutralism. In this context it is first asserted that a pain is what causes groaning, withdrawal, and other pain-behavior. Then it is pointed out that we might find—indeed, we expect to find—that groups of neurons firing in certain ways are such causes. In this way, it is concluded, we could get evidence for an identity view.[26]

The materials required for the reply to this objection are already present in the discussion of functionalism given above. Our concept of pain is not the same as the concept of whatever causes pain-behavior. For we also have knowledge about the causes of pain and

26. This objection is plausible for pains but not for afterimages, since there is no "yellow afterimage behavior", that is, no behavior that is characteristic of people who have yellow afterimages. (Reporting on afterimages is relatively rare, that is, *un*characteristic.) But then, pain is very frequently the example under discussion.

this enables us to understand how it is possible to bring about pain-behavior without causing pains. Therefore, showing that an item causes pain-behavior is not the same thing as showing that it is a pain. A possible reply to this is that I have misconstrued the topic-neutralist proposal and should have taken it to mean that a pain is what actually does cause pain-behavior in our world (and not merely whatever causes pain-behavior in whatever world we may be imagining).[27] This reading, however, makes the objection in the preceding paragraph question-begging. Let us agree with the proponent of the identity view that what causes pain-behavior are groups of firing neurons. Are these pains? All we are entitled to say is that *if* pains are identical with groups of firing neurons then they are causes of pain-behavior. This, naturally, gives us no reason to suppose that they are so identical. We may add that there is a familiar case, which we have already mentioned, that shows the objection to be mistaken on either reading. When people touch a hot stove their withdrawal (pain-behavior) precedes their pain. Thus the latter cannot be what causes the former.

There is one possible further source of confusion that it seems worthwhile to explore. To *explain* something is often just to give its causes. We can, of course, give explanations of this kind of why people have pains. In tracing the effects of stubbing a toe, for example, we would come upon the firings of neurons in the brain. These are causes of pains and thus they explain the pains, where "explain" means "give the causes of". However, this is not the kind of explaining that is required by the reducibility principle. In general, to explain *A*s by reference to the qualities and relations of their *constituents* is not to explain why *A*s occur by giving the causes of *A*s. Indeed, a constituent *could not* be a cause of that of which it is a

27. The difference between the two readings is the difference between taking "the cause of my pain" non-rigidly (first reading) and rigidly (second reading). See Saul Kripke, "Naming and Necessity", in Donald Davidson and Gilbert Harman, eds., *Semantics of Natural Language* (Dordrecht: Reidel, 1972).

constituent. Rather, to explain *A*s by reference to the qualities and relations of their constituents is to explain why such constituents *should be A*s. For example, when we say that water is piles of H_2O molecules, we are not expecting to answer the question "Why is there water here?" by reference to H_2O molecules. The kind of explanation demanded by the reducibility principle is an explanation of why piles of H_2O molecules should be water, that is, why it is that such piles should do all the things water observably does. Now, the key claim I have been making is that we have no idea why a group of neurons firing in this or that way *should be* a pain or an itch or a yellow afterimage and that we have no idea what would count as giving us this kind of explanation. The consequence is that we cannot supply what the reducibility principle requires for identity claims, when the identity proposed is between sensations and groups of firing neurons. The reducibility principle, however, is a sound principle. Therefore, sensations are not identical with groups of firing neurons.

Against Postulation

A dualistic view of sensations claims that sensations are not physical things. The identity view is by far the most popular way of disagreeing with such a dualism, but it is not the only way of doing so. In order to complete our defense of dualism we must now consider an alternative strategy, which has been proposed by Wilfrid Sellars. I have discussed Sellars' development of this proposal in detail elsewhere.[28] Here I must confine myself to a statement and criticism of its main idea. This involves an application of the method whereby particles are introduced into physics by postulating them as explanatory of recorded data.

Behind the postulation of particles in physics lies the following scenario. We may begin by imagining that we are accustomed to

28. See my "Sellarsian Materialism".

applying some theory (or, at least, that we have some expectation that certain regularities will hold). We now apply this theory to a new domain and are surprised to find that expected outcomes are not observed. A simple example of such a surprise can be envisaged if we imagine applying Newtonian mechanics to the motions of a collection of things that includes pith balls and rubber rods. Some of the motions of the pith balls will not be accountable for by the Newtonian rules. More sophisticated examples can be found in recent physics. As higher energies have become possible, predictions by old, lower-energy rules about the outcomes of bombardments have been found to be falsified. Now, the postulational response to surprises of this kind is to postulate that there is something that has certain properties and that, in virtue of those properties, explains the occurrence of the surprises. The result of this in the first example is the postulation of electrons with the property of negative charge. The result in the second example is quarks with their property of fractional charge.

Let us now consider the following parallel scenario. Our current neurophysiology has developed by applying physiology, chemistry, and physics to the material composing animal brains and central nervous systems. Many parts of the latter two sciences have been developed in contexts that are quite far removed from the conditions that give rise to sentient life. We are now to imagine that when we apply these sciences in ever more precise ways to animal brains, we are confronted by surprises. Neurons fire when not expected to and fail to fire when, according to current theory, they should. Stylus records fail to have the amplitudes and periodicity that we expected. We are further to imagine that we respond to these surprises with a theory that postulates pains and afterimages, tastes and smells, as having a role to play in the causation of neural activity. Finally, we are to imagine that this theory explains the hitherto surprising results and restores our ability to predict what goes on in animal brains.

This scenario is, of course, a very unlikely story. There is no evidence that breakdowns of the laws that apply to non-sentient things appear when we examine animal (including human) brains. The most that can be said for such a breakdown is that it can be given a coherent description, that is, it is indeed a logical possibility. Thus, those who would base their hopes for a successful anti-dualistic view on a postulational approach have *at best* a reason for thinking that anti-dualism *could be* true and no current evidence to suggest that it is actually true. However, even if the envisaged breakdown in our sciences were to occur we still would not really be entitled to conclude that sensations are physical. So, at least, I shall now argue.

We must begin by coming to a clear understanding of what is to count as *physical*. I shall follow Sellars in taking it to be a necessary and sufficient condition of a thing's being physical that it have a location in space.[29] If we are not to trivialize claims about physicality, however, we must take care to restrict the physical to what has spatial location in the most literal and non-derivative sense. Suppose now that some group of neurons fires in a certain pattern. Suppose this kind of occurrence is in violation of the laws of chemistry. Suppose further that we find such occurrences in people's brains on exactly those occasions when they have yellow afterimages. Suppose further that after long searching we can find no correlation between such occurrences and anything else. Then we *might* conclude that yellow afterimages caused groups of neurons to fire in this way. Even if we did so, however, this would not show that yellow afterimages are physical. This is because correlating the having of yellow afterimages and the having of certain neuron firings does not involve any assumption about spatial location of the for-

29. This usage corresponds to the "physical$_1$" of Paul Meehl and Wilfrid Sellars. See their paper "The Concept of Emergence", in Herbert Feigl and Michael Scriven, eds., *The Foundations of Science and the Concepts of Psychology and Psychoanalysis, Minnesota Studies in the Philosophy of Science*, vol. 1 (Minneapolis: University of Minnesota Press, 1956), p. 252.

mer. Consequently finding such a correlation gives no reason to assign any particular location to the afterimage.

To this it may be replied that sensations can be given location if the same postulation that gets them causally connected to neuron firings assigns them a location. This would mean that our "new" neurophysiology would have to have laws of the kind illustrated by this example: "Yellow afterimages have effects on neurons that decrease proportionately to the square of the distance." With such a law we could find where an afterimage is in the same way that we can determine the position of a planet by its gravitational effects.

It is very plausible to think that if a breakdown occurred in neurophysiology the problems thereby raised could be solved only by postulating things that would have properties with distance-dependent effects.[30] But the properties of being a pain, being a yellow afterimage, being a C♯ ringing in the ears, and so on do not have distance-dependent effects. Therefore it would not be things with *those* properties that would fulfill the role of restorers of neurophysiological predictability. The point being made here will be clearer if we emphasize that, according to the postulational scenario, the distance-dependent effects of sensations cannot be due merely to the properties of causes of sensations or to properties that happen to be correlated with pains, yellowness of afterimages, and so on. What the postulational scenario envisages—and what I am arguing is, in the end, unintelligible—is that a scientist may seriously propose that what makes a neuron fire is the yellowness of a nearby afterimage which, had it been blue, would not have made the neuron fire.

I assume that it will be conceded that sensations do not have any ordinary distance-dependent effects. For example, no one claims that things get warm when they are brought close to pains or heavier

30. "Property P has an effect E" is short for "The occurrence of things with the property P causes Es"—which in turn is to be understood to have the implication that if things of kind P had not been P, they would not have been followed by Es.

when moved toward patches of yellow. But it might be thought that one could discover that the properties of sensations had distance-dependent microeffects upon neurons. However, we have no model for a discovery of this kind. Properties like charge are *introduced as having* distance-dependent effects. They are not first known in some other way and then discovered to have such effects. We can imagine an anomaly-ridden neurophysiology being rescued by the postulation of things bearing *some* (newly introduced) property with distance-dependent effects. We cannot, however, imagine how we could have any reason to think that this newly introduced property was the same as any of the properties of sensations. In fact, we would always have a good reason to deny such an identity, since a connection with distance would be built into the concepts of newly introduced properties, whereas there is no such connection built into the concepts of pain, yellow, C♯, and so on.

This conclusion enables us to complete the argument of this subsection. Sensations cannot be given a spatial location by the postulational route; thus they cannot be established to be physical even in the unlikely case that they must be regarded as causes of neural firings. With this result we have finished considering the ways that seemed to provide an argument for the physicality of sensations. The upshot has been similar in both cases. When you try to take seriously the idea that a sensation is a physical thing, when you try to imagine in detail, for a particular case, how the physicalist story is supposed to go, you find that you have to propose to yourself something that is not fully intelligible.

Epiphenomenalism

In the preceding section I considered a scenario involving a breakdown in the predictive success of contemporary neurophysiology. I recognized such a breakdown as being logically possible. I also imagined possible developments that might show that sensations caused groups of neurons to fire in some definite pattern. I have been indulgent about these possibilities because I think it is important to see that even if we allow them we do not get a way of understanding how sensations could be physical. I now wish to emphasize, however, that we have no direct reason for believing these possibilities to be actual. Quite the contrary: there have been many successes of neural science in understanding the structure and operations of neurons and synapses. Every such success is evidence that physics and chemistry can describe sufficient causes of neural firings and that sensations need not be called upon to fill any causal gaps.

There is, however, a line of argument that has convinced some that we must allow for causation by sensations and that therefore we must allow for such causal gaps. It is not that these philosophers take lightly the riskiness of anticipating what scientific investigation will eventually discover. Instead, they believe they have found a reason within science itself that demands such a conclusion.[31] The science that they believe supports this position is evolutionary biology. The connections that are crucial to their case can be brought out by the following argument. Like Puccetti, I have used the plausible example of pain.

(1) The theory of evolution is true.
(2) The theory of evolution implies that characteristics regularly possessed in a species must have (or have had) survival value.
(3) Having pains is a characteristic regularly possessed in some species. Therefore,
(4) Pains have (or have had) survival value.
(5) Nothing has survival value unless it affects behavior. Therefore,
(6) Pains have (or have had) behavioral effects.

31. A very clear statement of the argument occurs in R. Puccetti, "Is Pain Necessary?" *Philosophy* 50 (1975): 259–269. See also Karl Popper in his and J. C. Eccles' *The Self and Its Brain* (New York: Springer-Verlag, 1977), pp. 72–74.

I shall assume that if pains have behavioral effects, they have them through affecting the firings of neurons connected (directly or indirectly) to the motor system. I shall also assume that if pains once had behavioral effects they still do have them.

Anyone who accepts the foregoing argument will want to go on to ask how pains can have behavioral effects. Just two answers present themselves. One is that pains are identical with groups of firing neurons and that they thus can have their effects through the electrochemical means studied and explained in neuroscience. The other is that pains are non-physical but make a causal contribution to some neural firings.

Despite my rejection of the identity claim presupposed by the first answer, I do not accept this second position. The reason is that I believe we cannot legitimately get as far as line (6) above. The problem is that premise (2) is false. To get a true statement (2) must be modified at least as far as (2').

(2') The theory of evolution implies that characteristics regularly possessed in a species must *either* have (or have had) survival value *or* be nomologically connected to those that do.

From this, however, we can only get the conclusion that pains either cause(d) behavior or are nomologically connected to such causes.

I believe that a small amount of reflection will make it evident that (2) has to be modified in the way suggested and that this formally removes the force of the stated argument. But to remove entirely the suspicion that there is something to the suggested appeal to evolution, we must call attention to the following key fact. Evolutionary theory contains no explanation whatsoever as to why any particular kind of group of neurons firing in some way should cause a pain. Even if we were to suppose that natural selection favors creatures in which some neural structures cause pains, that would only explain why certain creatures survive and not why certain neural structures cause pains. But in fact we cannot even get the suggested explanation. For what is relevant to evolution is that certain inputs I (for example, tissue damage) should be connected to certain outputs O (for example, withdrawal). This end is served just as well by the arrangements in each of the following hypotheses.

(H_1) I causes neural ephemeral individual b_1, which causes a pain and another such individual, b_2. b_2 then causes O.

(H_2) I causes b_1, as in (H_1). b_1 causes only a pain. The pain causes b_2. b_2 then causes O.

Since I and O are equally connected under these hypotheses, Nature has, so to speak, no interest in which one holds; so it cannot select the arrangement in one over the arrangement in the other. It is no use to say that since we have pains, they must be efficacious, that is, (H_2) must be true. For since evolutionary theory has nothing to say about what neural firings should produce what sensations, it has nothing to say against the possibility that the thing needed to produce b_2 on appropriate occasions—that is, b_1—is the very thing that also produces pain. That is, it has nothing to say against (H_1).

In the absence of a reason why we *have* to accept (H_2), it would be unreasonable to do so. This is because in order to accept it we would have to declare a limitation on well-established general laws; that is, we would have to declare that there will someday be discovered a breakdown in the application of physics and chemistry to neuronal tissue. It is not reasonable to do this in the absence of actual evidence of breakdown.

Now, there is a position that holds out the promise of being able to accept the conclusion of the argument based on evolution while avoiding the need to suppose that there will be a breakdown of the kind just described. This view concedes that physical science shows us causes of a kind that are sufficient to produce every occurrence in the brain. It holds, however, that sensations can be supposed *also* to be causes of such occurrences, *without* having to be supposed to be physical. One of the more plausible arguments for this view rests on three premises.[32] The first is that sensations are caused by some groups of neurons firing in certain ways. The second is that sensations have only one physical cause. This premise hardly seems compelling. It is not evident why there could not be two kinds of firing patterns in groups of neurons that would both produce pains or afterimages or ringings in the ears that would be indistinguishable from each other. However, whether or not this can happen is an empirical question. In the present discussion I shall simply concede the premise—that is, I shall assume that each kind of sensation has but one neural cause—in order clearly to bring out the conceptual difficulties in the remainder of the argument. The third premise is that where there is law-like regularity there is causation. Let us make explicit how these premises are supposed to lead to a causal role for sensations.

Let b_2 be an (ephemeral) individual consisting of some group of neurons firing in a certain way. For this discussion we are assuming that such individuals have physical causes. We may suppose that the cause of b_2 is another individual consisting of some other group of neurons, which occurs a little before b_2. Let us call this cause "b_1". Let us further suppose that b_1 also causes a sensation, S, and that there is no other cause of that kind of sensation. Finally, let us suppose that these three things begin to exist in the temporal order b_1, then S, then b_2. (By picking an effect of b_1 that is late enough, we can ensure that it begins to exist after S.) Since the connection be-

32. A. I. Goldman has given a clear statement of the argument to be discussed below. See his "The Compatibility of Mechanism and Purpose", *Philosophical Review* 78 (1969): 468–482. Cf. my discussion of his argument in "Do Pains Make a Difference to Our Behavior?" *American Philosophical Quarterly* 16 (1979): 327–334.

tween b_1 and b_2 is causal, b_1 is regularly followed by b_2.[33] Since b_1 is the only cause of S, S is regularly preceded by b_1. It follows that S is regularly followed by b_2. By the third of the above premises, and the assumed temporal order, it follows further that S causes b_2.

The third of the above premises, however, is false. What is true is that where there is causation there must be law-like regularity. It is also true that *usually* where there is law-like regularity there is causation. There are, however, exceptions to this rule. In fact, there is a whole class of exceptions of which the above case is a member. What is distinctive of this class is that the regularity of, say, z and y is a dependent one, that is, dependent on regularities between z and x, and x and y. Let us have another illustration of this situation. Depressing the plunger on my camera ($= x$) does two things. It unlocks the winding mechanism ($= z$) so that the film may be advanced. It also causes the shutter to move ($= y$). Further, the only thing that unlocks the winding mechanism is depressing the plunger. I don't know whether these things happen in the order x, y, z in my camera, but it would be easy to construct a camera in which they did occur in that order. It would also be easy to ensure that the plunger works "digitally", that is, in such a way that there is no possibility of depressing it part way, so as to bring about y but not z. Under these conditions it would be true that the winding mechanism is unlocked if and only if the shutter has moved. This would be a law-like regularity. We would be entitled to the counterfactual "If the shutter had not moved, the winding mechanism would not have been unlocked." Clearly, however, it would *not* be true that the winding mechanism was unlocked *because* the shutter moved. The reason is obviously that the regularity that would be required behind such a causal connection is dependent on other connections and these

---

33. "x is regularly followed by y" is short for "Things of the kind that x is are regularly followed by things of the kind that y is." Of course, the kinds involved must be causally relevant ones. For an explanation of the causal relevance of kinds, see above, note 30.

other connections do all the causal work that we have any reason to suppose is present. Now this is exactly the situation that holds with b_1 (= x), S (= y), and b_2 (= z). Thus we are not entitled to say that S causes b_2.

I want to emphasize that we *are* entitled to the Counterfactual

(CF)   If S had not occurred, b_2 would not have occurred.

There is a powerful temptation to move from this to the Causal Claim

(CC) S caused b_2.

Additional features of many cases do enable us to move from claims like (CF) to claims like (CC). Such cases are so familiar that such a move is nearly automatic. For this reason, the most plausible way of presenting the view I am criticizing is to begin with the counterfactual claim. Despite all this, it should be clear from the preceding paragraph that the move from the first of these claims, taken by itself, to the second is fallacious.

I have been criticizing a line of reasoning whose intended result is that sensations can be causes of occurrences in the brain even though those occurrences have sufficient physical causes. We can go further and argue that any attempt of this kind must fail. If there is a sufficient physical cause for a neuron or group of neurons to fire, then a fully satisfactory story about the causes of those firings could (in principle) be told and it could be told in terms that are entirely physical. If we had such a story, there could be no occasion on which we could improve our science of the brain by bringing in sensations as causes. With no causal gaps in our physical account, there could never be a good reason to prefer one mechanism by which sensations might (redundantly) cause neural firings to any other such mechanism. With no reason to propose one mechanism rather than another for the means by which a sensation could cause neural firings, and no lack of sufficient (physical) conditions for them, there would be nothing even to suggest that sensations are causes of neural firings—except, of course, the regular co-occurrence of kinds of sensations and kinds of neural firing patterns. We have just argued, however, that since this regularity is a dependent one, it does not afford a good reason for asserting causal connection.

In the previous section, I argued that sensations *might* reasonably be considered to be causes of occurrences in the brain *if* there were a breakdown in our physical sciences when we applied them to brains. That is to say, if there were a neural firing for which we could not find a sufficient physical cause, then it might be reasonable to say that sensations have a causal role to play in what goes on in the brain. I also argued that even in this case we should not be led to alter our previous conclusion that sensations are not physical. In the present section I have argued that we have neither a direct nor an indirect way of making it reasonable to suppose that there is such a breakdown. I have argued further that in the absence of such a breakdown there can be no reasonable way of holding that sensations are causes of neural firings. If we put all these conclusions together, we can see that it is not reasonable to hold that sensations are physical or to attribute to them a causal role in determining our neural firings or our behavior. We are left with the view that sensations are non-physical and non-efficacious.

In traditional terminology, this view is known as "epiphenomenalism". Epiphenomenalism has rather a bad name. The reasons for this bad name come down to two major objections, which I shall now explain and examine.

Objections and Replies

Knowing Sensations

In ordinary cases of seeing a tree, the tree causes light to be reflected, which causes changes in the retina. These changes cause neurons to fire, which in turn cause us to believe there is a tree in the direction we are looking. Looking, and seeing a tree, is the ordinary way of getting to know that there is a tree over there. It is essential to this kind of knowing that the belief be causally dependent on the tree. If such a connection is not present, we may have a lucky guess, but not knowledge.

Perceptual knowledge is often taken as the model for all knowledge. Thus are spawned, for example, "introspection" and "the eye of the mind". Because of this it is easy to come to believe that the following principle about Causation and Knowledge is true:

(CK)   Knowledge requires the known to cause something in the knower.

The combination of this principle with epiphenomenalism results immediately in the conclusion that sensations cannot be known. This conclusion is both manifestly false and inconsistent with the assertion of epiphenomenalism. Thus the natural outcome of accepting (CK) is the rejection of epiphenomenalism. I shall argue, however, that (CK) is strictly false, since it does not hold for the case of sensations. The key to showing this lies in the observation that, if (CK) were true, then allowing for sensations to have neural effects should make a difference to their knowability. My strategy will be to show that allowing for such effects in fact makes no difference to the knowability of sensations.

Since there are several relations we must keep track of, it will be helpful to diagram them. Figure 1 represents a case of a sensation, S,

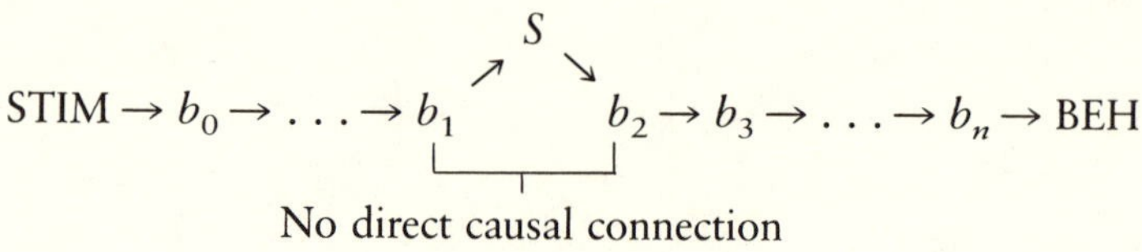

$$\text{STIM} \rightarrow b_0 \rightarrow \ldots \rightarrow b_1 \overset{S}{\underset{\underset{\text{No direct causal connection}}{\rule{3cm}{0.4pt}}}{\nearrow \searrow}} b_2 \rightarrow b_3 \rightarrow \ldots \rightarrow b_n \rightarrow \text{BEH}$$

Figure 1

causing neural firings in the only way we have been able to conceive this as possible. Here, b_1 and b_2 are as in the preceding section. Also as above, S is regularly followed by b_2. b_0, b_3, and b_n are groups of neurons firing in some way, coming in the indicated positions in the causal series. Arrows represent causal relations. STIM is some stimulation of neurons that have their ends in a sense organ. BEH is some behavior resulting from muscle contractions caused by b_n. (BEH might be, for example, withdrawing from a painful object, but it includes reporting on one's sensations.) In order to ensure a causal role for S, we must assume, first, that our scientific laws do not lead us to predict b_2 after b_1. This alone, however, would leave open the possibility that b_1 is as highly correlated with b_2 as S is. In this case, despite the breakdown of physical theory, we would have as much reason to call b_1 the cause of b_2 as we would to call S the cause of b_2. To avoid this we must suppose that there are things other than b_1 that cause S and that are not connected by our physical theories to the occurrence of b_2. This arrangement would give us as much reason as we could possibly have for saying that S causes b_2.

Let us now focus our attention on b_3 and on BEH. Let us take as our example of the latter a report that I have a pain. The question we must ask is, What is the connection between b_3 and the fact that my report expresses my knowledge that I have a pain? One thing is clear: the connection does *not* lie in the fact that b_3 is caused by a sensation, since it isn't; it is caused by b_2. What does seem relevant to the connection of b_3 with knowledge is just the following. (i) b_3 would not have occurred unless the pain, S, had occurred. That is, b_3 is a reliable indicator of the recent presence of S. (It is not actually represented in the diagram that b_3 has no other way of being produced except by b_2. Let us add this assumption. If one thought that b_3 might be caused in some other way, one would come to regard the connection between S and BEH as too tenuous to support the claim that my pain-report expresses knowledge.) (ii) If b_3 were not a cause of my pain-report it could not help explain why that report expresses knowledge. For example, if all b_3 did was to raise my blood pressure, it would just not come into the account of how it happens that my report is true when I utter it. Thus, possessing a role in the production of my pain-report is required if b_3 is to have anything to do with knowledge. Now, these two points are the only ones that connect b_3 with knowledge. I cannot, of course, prove that these are the only relevant points. I am, however, at a loss to see what else could be thought to be relevant.

Let us now look at a case of having and reporting on a sensation, as this is portrayed by epiphenomenalism. The same conventions used above produce Figure 2. The crucial point to notice is that *the same knowledge-relevant features that were possessed by* b_3 *on the previous view are possessed by it on this view.* This shows that the status of the sensation report BEH as knowledge is independent of whether or not S has neural effects. It is, of course, important that our view ensure the truth of

(CF′)   If S had not occurred, the report that it occurred
        would not have been made.

We have seen, however, that this does not entail

(CC′)   S caused the report that it occurred to be made.

We have also seen that (CF′) is as well supported by epiphenomenalism, which denies (CC′), as it is by the view represented in Figure 1.

The criticism of epiphenomenalism to which I have been responding has recently been given an intriguing formulation by D. C. Den-

$$\text{STIM} \to b_0 \to \ldots \to b_1 \overset{\nearrow S}{\longrightarrow} b_2 \to b_3 \to \ldots \to b_n \to \text{BEH}$$

Figure 2

nett. I believe it will clarify and deepen our understanding of the point I have been making to see how it applies to Dennett's formulation. This goes as follows:

> [T]he postulation of the non-physical effects [i.e., epiphenomenal sensations] is utterly idle, for *ex hypothesi* were the effects to cease to occur (other things remaining the same), people would go right on making the same sorts of introspective claims, avowing their pains and taking as much aspirin as ever. Even more vividly, were a person's epiphenomena to be gradually delayed until they ran, say, ten years behind her physical life, she and we could never discover this![34]

The easiest way to bring out what is wrong with this argument is to consider an analogous argument directed against an identity theorist, and such a theorist's reply. The argument is this:

> The postulation of pains as identical with neuron firings is utterly idle, for *ex hypothesi* were pains to cease to be identical with those neuron firings people would go right on making the same sorts of introspective claims, avowing their pains and taking as much aspirin as ever.

The obvious reply to this argument is that the supposition that is thought to lead to the absurd consequence does not make sense. For it is *necessarily* true that if A and B are identical, they must remain so and cannot come to be non-identical. This is a sufficient and compelling reply. The epiphenomenalist, however, has a precisely analogous reply to the argument quoted from Dennett. The supposition of this argument that is thought to lead to absurdity is that what causes non-physical effects might at some time cease to do so. This does not make sense. It is *necessarily* true that if As cause Bs, As must continue to

---

34. D. C. Dennett, "Current Issues in Philosophy of Mind", *American Philosophical Quarterly* 15 (1978): 252. An earlier version of the discussion to follow appears in my "Causation, Sensations and Knowledge", *Mind* 91 (1982): 524–540.

cause Bs and cannot come no longer to do so. If we were to find future As not causing future Bs (presumably by finding future As not followed by Bs) we would conclude that, after all, it was not (and never had been) As (or As alone) that caused Bs.

This point can be overlooked in the context of the original argument because the epiphenomenalist makes another, related claim that is indeed contingent, namely, the claim that physical things (groups of neurons firing) cause pains. However, Dennett's objection cannot turn on a rejection of this claim; that would merely make it question-begging. Further, the objection cannot turn on the idea that this causal connection *might* not have obtained, for to this the epiphenomenalist can quite happily agree.

There is an alternative way of taking Dennett's argument that we will now explore. This interpretation starts with the observation that a given effect may be able to be brought about in more than one way. This observation may suggest the following picture. At present, we suppose, b_1 brings about both pain and b_2. (See Figure 2.) But, we further suppose, b_2 may be brought about by something else, say b_1'. Now, b_1' may not also cause pain; and if it does not then it could happen, after all, that we might come to have (and thus, may have already come to have) all our pain-behavior without any pains. Happily, from the epiphenomenalist's point of view, this picture fails to lead where Dennett would wish, namely to the view that we cannot discover our mistake. For, since b_1' has properties different from those of b_1, it is not contradictory to suppose that b_1' will have some differences in its effects besides the sole one of not causing pain. For example, b_1' might initiate a causal chain leading to a declaration at some later time that one has been exhibiting pain-behavior without any pain. Of course, this outcome *may* not happen, and thus epiphenomenalists have to admit that a certain kind of deception is possible. They need not, however, admit that they *must* fail to detect change in the manner of causation of pain-behavior.

The admission that such a change *might* escape notice according to epiphenomenalism is no objection to that view, because analogous failures are constructible on any view. Let us consider just two. (i) Suppose occurrences of b_1 are identical with pains and are what cause occurrences of b_2. Suppose further that occurrences of b_2 start being generally brought about by occurrences of b_1' rather than of b_1. Then there will no longer be pains connected with b_2 and pain-reports caused by b_2 will be false. But the change in causation of occurrences of b_2 might go undetected. (ii) Suppose that a pain is just whatever it is that produces pain-behaviors. Suppose further that b_1 performs this function for a time but then b_1' replaces b_1 in this capacity. Then, of course, we cannot say that we now have pain-behaviors without pains. But we will have to say something analogous, namely, that what pains are has changed without our noticing this. We can say, further, that it might turn out that we come to discover this change, but then again we might be forever unaware of it.

There is a natural reply to the foregoing discussion that it is easy to imagine Dennett making. Since it exhibits his central contention in its most plausible form, it is both helpful and necessary to state this rejoinder and confront it directly.

I will grant (says our imaginary Dennett) that *if* you *knew* that epiphenomenalism were true, you would be entitled to defend the view as you have. But the difficulty with your discussion is precisely that it question-beggingly supposes it to be possible both that epiphenomenalism is true *and* that we know that it is. The trouble with epiphenomenalism is that we might have the very same reasons for it that we now have, even if it were false; and therefore we do not know that it is true. Alternatively, epiphenomenalism is compatible with our having the same reasons for saying that we have pains that we actually do have, even if there were no pains; and so, once again, if epiphenomenalism were true, we would not know we had pains.

This rejoinder rests on one of two assumptions, neither of which we ought to accept. The first assumption I shall discuss is the view that

(A_1) If I know I am in pain, I must believe that my being in pain causally contributes to my believing I am in pain.

The easiest way to see that this is wrong is to imagine a case in which I have been injured and am holding myself, yelling and complaining how much I hurt. Evidently, I do not believe that pains causally contribute to pain-beliefs and my being injured would not make me come to believe this. So anyone who accepts (A_1) ought to say that, in the case described, I would not know that I was in pain. This, however, is an extremely counterintuitive result. Of course, if I believed this statement:

(S_1) I would believe that I have a pain whether or not I actually had one

then one might well doubt that I *know* I have a pain. But it should be quite obvious by now that I can deny (S_1) without having to believe that pains cause anything.

The other assumption that might be at work in giving plausibility to the rejoinder we have imagined Dennett to make is

(A_2) If I know I am in pain, the pain must causally contribute to my believing I am in pain.

This, however, is merely (CK) particularized as to knower, type of sensation, and type of effect; and we have already shown why we should not accept (CK).

Sensations and Actions

The objection we are now to consider begins in some obvious common sense truths, for example, "I removed the splinter because it hurt" and "I put the cheese away very promptly because it stank."

The fact that such remarks are sometimes true appears to commit one to recognizing sensations as causes of actions. Thus epiphenomenalism, which denies that sensations causally contribute to actions, seems to be in conflict with common sense.

I shall argue that this conflict is only apparent.[35] The cases in which we do things "because of" sensations are just the cases in which we act with the intention of causing a sensation to cease or to continue, or to increase or decrease in intensity. Having such an intention does not require sensations to have effects. It does require having the belief that one has the sensations one is trying to further or hinder; but we can take the preceding subsection as showing that this condition can be met without assigning any effects to sensations. It also requires that one be prepared, other things being equal, to do what one believes will further or hinder one's sensation. This again one can have without supposing that sensations cause anything. The materials for the argument for this have already been given. All the effects of a sensation represented in Figure 1 above are present in Figure 2, in which the sensation is not efficacious. These effects include the neural firings that lead to behavior that is designed to further or hinder a sensation. Therefore the required behavior is as much to be expected on the epiphenomenalist view as on any other.

The view that acting "because of" sensations is really acting with the intention of affecting our sensations finds some support in the following fact. When we make the kinds of common sense remarks mentioned above we rely only on believing that people have a sensation and that they are doing what they think will further or hinder it. Of course, it is not always trivial to establish these things. For example, there may be more important things at hand than comfort and so intentions to, say, get rid of a splinter as soon as one has a

35. A more detailed version of this argument can be found in my "Do Pains Make a Difference to our Behavior?" pp. 330–333.

chance may not be evident to anyone else. Or we may have to change our opinion of someone who is wrapping cheese when we find out that she has a cold and is thus temporarily deprived of most olfactory sensations. However, once we have established the presence of a sensation and an appropriate tendency of action, we do not require anything further to feel entirely justified in saying that a person is acting because of that sensation. We do not undertake causal investigations about sensations, nor do we feel deprived of relevant evidence because we do not do so.

This is the only direct way of supporting the view that acting because of a sensation is really acting in order to further or hinder it. There are, however, some sources of indirect support. One lies in the fact that there are numerous other cases in which "because" is clearly rephraseable into "in order to". If I go to the store because the beer ran out, I go in order to replenish the beer supply. If I stay home because a blizzard is coming, I stay home in order to avoid the perils of such weather. If I refrain from insulting you because our host wouldn't like it, I refrain in order not to offend our host. Moreover, there is good reason to believe that rephrasing the "because" idiom into the language of purposes is the right thing to do when dealing with the schema "*P* did *A* because of a sensation *S*." We do not really think of people as behaving simply in response to sensations. We do not expect to find simple regularities connecting the presence of a sensation with some one type of action. Rather, what we do about bad smells, sunsets, itches, and even most pains is controllable and subject to our beliefs about what will further or hinder them, what it is polite to do, and what other purposes we have. These facts suggest that sensations are involved in actions as objects of our desires or aversions rather than as causes.

It may be thought that significant pain provides an exception to this conclusion. That is, it may seem that pain causes groans and that "He groaned because he was in pain" cannot be paraphrased into the "He groaned in order to . . ." style. To reply to this point we must begin by considering reflexes. We have already mentioned that withdrawal from a hot stove begins before the pain from touching it is felt. This fact has a natural explanation. The withdrawal is produced by a reflex arc that involves neurons running from, for example, the hand to the spinal cord, from one point to another within the spinal cord, and from the spinal cord to muscles in the hand. Pain, however, is not felt until the neural signal from the hand has been propagated to the brain. This explanation reinforces the conclusion, already drawn on phenomenal grounds, that the pain is not a cause of the withdrawal. Now, in so far as groaning occurs as a reflex there is no reason why we should not regard it in the same way as a withdrawal from a hot stove. There are, however, groans and groans. Not all of them can plausibly be taken to be reflexes. One can sometimes make one's pain a little less by tightening one's visceral muscles. Doing so is a fully intentional action even though nearly automatic. Such tightening tends to force air out of the lungs. To prevent this from happening (it would leave one without air and the visceral muscles soon would have to be relaxed to permit breathing) one closes one's throat. If one does not do this quite completely, the result is a groan. These non-reflex groans are thus side effects caused by something that one does in order to (slightly) relieve one's pain. This explains why certain kinds of pain regularly go with groaning without supposing that the pain is a cause of groaning. It also explains why paraphrase into purposive language does not work in this case. One tightens one's muscles because of the pain, that is, in order to relieve it; the groaning is an unintended side effect. That one can, if need be, suppress this side effect does not, of course, show that it is intended when it does occur.

With this conclusion we have reached the end of our introduction of sensations as ephemeral individuals and our defense of the claims that they are not physical, that they are not efficacious, that we know them, and that reference to them characterizes some of our purposes. It is, of course, too soon to expect final acceptance of the view that sensations are ephemeral individuals; that, as I indicated, must await the coherent resolution of several further questions. I shall, however, be taking it as established that *if* sensations are ephemeral individuals, then the other claims listed above are correct.

Some of the further issues we must consider concern the relation of sensations to our conceptual abilities. Some of these can be taken up directly and will be discussed in the next chapter. Some issues, however, must await further developments, in particular the discussion of intentionality. In Chapter V we will be concerned in part with showing how the accounts of sensations and of intentionality fit into an account of one whole self. It is also there that we will explore the temptation to introduce an act-object analysis of sensations and make good on the promise not to succumb to it. However, not all of our further references to topics discussed in the present chapter will concern problems to be worked out. In Chapter III and again in Chapter V, we will extend the range of the key argument against the identity of sensations with groups of firing neurons. This will provide important parts of the solutions to certain problems. In Chapter VI, we will be able to see the importance of the fact that the pursuit and avoidance of sensations enters into our purposes.

CHAPTER II

Certainty

The concern that philosophers have had for certainty spans a number of different issues. In some contexts, however, claims about certainty have long been inextricably bound up with claims about sensations. This connection has been so close that my account may be thought to be unclear or incomplete unless I explain the relations between sensations and some issues about certainty. One of the aims of the present chapter is to provide the required explanations. I shall, however, be concerned with a broader purpose. To know something is not the same as to have a sensation—even when what is known is that one is having some kind of sensation. Knowing involves believing and we shall find in the next chapter that believing requires a treatment quite different from that of sensations. This difference leads to some natural questions about how the two accounts fit together. If we are to have the coherent, unified account of human mental capacity at which this book aims, these questions must be answered. The discussions of the present chapter will accomplish part of this task.

Appearances

Many philosophers have approached the subject of sensations by discussing illusions and hallucinations. Some very familiar cases are square towers, which appear round from a distance; oars, which appear bent when stuck into water; and pink rats, which have been imagined to appear to consumers of mood-altering drugs. These examples give rise to a characteristic Argument from Illusion, which may be represented as follows:

(AI) In cases of illusions and hallucinations, something has a certain property (for example, being round, having straight parts joined at an angle, being pink and rat-shaped).

In these same cases there is no physical object that has those properties and that is affecting the sense organs. Therefore,

In these cases there is an "internal" thing that has those properties and that we know about in some way other than ordinary perception.

Let us call the special items arrived at in the conclusion of this argument "appearances". We can then restate the conclusion as the claim that there are appearances of various kinds. It is natural to go on to argue that appearances are not identical with parts of one's body and that therefore they are not physical objects at all. Strictly speaking, however, this is an additional argument.

It will come as no surprise that I believe that there are appearances and that these are nothing but sensations. To describe something as an appearance is, however, to say more than that it is a sensation. First, we reserve the term "appearance" for cases in which the sensation is of a kind that is at least very like noticing a property of a physical thing. Thus, pains and itches are not ordinarily called "appearances". Second, the term "appearance" suggests a contrast with what really is the case. We *can* talk about the appearance that something presents when it is really there and when we make no mistake about it. We can do so because we can have two sensations of the same kind caused in different ways, for example, by a bent oar in air or a straight one half in water. But many uses of "appearance" carry the weight of "mere appearance". That is, they imply that the sensation that is being called "an appearance" is one that usually has a certain kind of cause, and would usually be a noticing of some property of a physical thing, but is being brought about in this case in some unusual way.

Although I accept the conclusion of (AI) I regard it as much too simple an argument. Its first premise assumes that properties enter into illusions by being properties of individual things. This is correct, but we have seen that this is a point that requires argument. (AI) is also defective because it only points toward and does not really articulate the fundamental point that afterimages, noticings of the properties of things, and appearances can all be literally similar in respects such as color and shape.

So far in this section I have merely related the view developed in Chapter I to talk about appearances and to (AI). I want now to consider two objections to what I have been saying. Both allege, in effect, that I have misconstrued the contexts in which we talk about appearances and that to account for those contexts we do not need to bring in sensations. The first of these objections comes from Gilbert Ryle. According to Ryle, all reports about how things appear or seem are merely guarded perceptual reports.[1] That is, they assert that something is perceived, but they assert this with less than full confidence. On this view, all reports of the form "x appears F" are tantamount to "I perceive x to be F—I think." This view, however, is clearly wrong. There are, of course, *some* claims about appearing that fit Ryle's description. Thus, for example, "It looks like three men are coming across the field" is roughly equivalent to "I think I see three men coming across the field." But there are many reports

1. See Gilbert Ryle, "Sensation", in R. J. Swartz, *Perceiving, Sensing, and Knowing* (Garden City, N.Y.: Doubleday, 1965), pp. 187–203.

about how things appear to which this equivalence does not apply. I can accuse the coffee of being so weak as to look like tea without for a moment thinking or asserting, however, weakly, that it may *be* tea. I can say that it smells like dead leaves in here without asserting at all that there are dead leaves in here. There are an indefinitely large number of examples of this kind.

If statements about how things appear really were guarded perceptual reports there could be no point in asserting them after one had arrived at a view in which one had full confidence. Consider, for example, Sellars' blue tie that looks green indoors under electric lighting.[2] If "This looks green" really had the force of "(I see that) this is green—I think" it would hardly be rational to say that the tie looks green if one were convinced it was blue. Yet the natural thing that people say in such a case is that a tie, which they know to be blue because they have taken it outside, looks green inside the tie shop.

The second objection to my treatment of appearances is derived from Richard Rorty. According to Rorty,

> The fact that "seems to seem . . ." is an expression without a use is a fact about the notion of "appearance," not a tip-off to the presence of "phenomenal properties." For the appearance-reality distinction is not based on a distinction between subjective representations and objective states of affairs; it is merely a matter of getting something wrong, having a false belief.[3]

There is something that is correct about this, namely that we would not have the concept of appearances that we have unless we believed that there could be misleading and false appearances. It does not follow, however, that the appearance-reality distinction is *merely* a

2. Cf. Wilfrid Sellars, *Science, Perception and Reality* (New York: Humanities Press, 1963), pp. 142–144.

3. Richard Rorty, *Philosophy and the Mirror of Nature* (Princeton, N.J.: Princeton University Press, 1979), p. 77.

matter of false belief or that it does not in some way involve "subjective representations", that is, sensations. It is in fact obvious that false belief is not all there is to the appearance-reality distinction. The tie example is a case in point. It makes good sense to say that it appears other than it is, that is, green, even when the clerk tells us immediately that it is blue, so that we never have a false belief about it. Again, the Muller-Lyer lines still look unequal even when we are fully informed about the nature of this illusion and thus believe them to be equal. Again, when we run cold water on our half-frozen hands, it feels warm; but there is no need to imagine that we are deceived into thinking that the water *is* warm.

Someone might be tempted to argue that Rorty's objection stands because in these counterexamples the appearances *could* have been misleading, or even *would* have been so had not experience forearmed us with the proper defenses against error. The observation is correct, but it is no support for Rorty's position. The reason is that the same connection between appearances and possible error is to be expected on the view I have been articulating, which recognizes appearances. To support Rorty's view, one would have to hold that sensations contribute nothing to talk about appearances and that such talk derives *solely* from a connection with possible error. This, however, seems dubious. Consider, for example, the gambler's fallacy, the fact that students often confuse the truth of a hypothetical with the truth of its antecedent, and the fact that a question posed with a double or triple negative will tend to be answered less successfully than one that is straightforwardly phrased. In these cases we have proneness to error by those who have not learned to be wary, *without* the presence of any relevant sensations. In these cases we also do *not* find people speaking of misleading appearances. Thus, these cases support the view that talk of misleading appearances does not reflect the possibility of error by itself, but comes in where the possibility or likelihood of error is due to there being sensations caused in atypical ways.

Incorrigibility

Many philosophers who have accepted the view that there are appearances have claimed that people can have incorrigible knowledge about their own appearances. Those who have taken this view have also regarded other sensations in the same way; that is, they have claimed that we have incorrigible knowledge of all our sensations. It is typical for those who make this claim to allow that we can misspeak so that, for example, we may have a green sensation while claiming to have a brown one, even when we are not lying. This, however, is regarded as "verbal error" and is not taken to be in conflict with the claim that we have incorrigible knowledge of our sensations.

There have also been many philosophers who have denied that we have incorrigible knowledge of our sensations.[4] In order to determine whether they are right we must get clearer about what incorrigibility amounts to. The first point we must notice is that incorrigibilism may be stated positively or negatively. The positive view is that we always know what kind of sensation we are having. When this view is accepted, sensations are sometimes called "self-intimating". The negative view is that we cannot be genuinely mistaken about what kind of sensation we are having. "Genuine" mistake is, of course, to be contrasted with verbal mistake. These two views are, as we shall see, distinct and they require different treatments. We will begin with the positive view. Its evaluation requires that we say a little more about knowing one's sensations.

4. See, e.g., Paul Meehl, "The Compleat Autocerebroscopist", in P. K. Feyerabend and Grover Maxwell, eds., *Mind, Matter, and Method: Essays in Philosophy and Science in Honor of Herbert Feigl* (Minneapolis: University of Minnesota Press, 1966); D. M. Armstrong, *A Materialist Theory of the Mind* (London: Routledge & Kegan Paul, 1968); K. P. Parsons, "Mistaking Sensations", *Philosophical Review* 79 (1970): 201–213; J. H. Chandler, "Incorrigibility and Classification", *Australasian Journal of Philosophy* 48 (1970): 101–106; and J. L. Austin, *Sense and Sensibilia*, ed. G. J. Warnock (New York: Oxford University Press, 1964).

To know that one has a sensation of a particular kind, one must at least understand the words in which the claim to have that kind of sensation would be expressed. Such understanding requires an indefinitely large number of abilities.[5] For example, children are not credited with knowing what "pain" means until they apply it to themselves and to others when obvious injuries have occurred. They must also realize that people wish to avoid having pains and that one can have pains without obvious injuries. Understanding "yellow" requires that daisies and egg yolks are classified as yellow and that cardinals are not. It also requires one to realize that a yellow thing could be seen under conditions in which it would not look yellow, for example, at dusk or in the darkroom with only a red light.

If we put these remarks together with our discussions in the latter half of Chapter I, we arrive at the view that people know that they have a sensation of a kind K only if (i) they have a sensation of kind K; (ii) they are disposed to describe their sensation, under some conditions or other; (iii) their being disposed as in (ii) is a causal consequence of the causes of the sensation; and (iv) they understand the words involved in the report that, according to (ii), they are disposed to give under some conditions. It follows from this that it is possible to have a sensation but not to know anything about it—for (i) could be satisfied even if (ii)–(iv) are not. Thus, if "Sensations are self-intimating" is taken to imply the necessary truth of "If a sensation is had by a person, that person knows what kind of sensation it is", then sensations are not self-intimating. However, I suspect that most incorrigibilists would be prepared to give up the positive, self-intimation view once they see that it is really distinct from the negative view. I shall now turn to this other claim.

I shall proceed by describing some cases that do *not* involve claims about sensations. I shall then compare these cases and con-

5. Cf. Carl Ginet, "How Words Mean Kinds of Sensations", *Philosophical Review* 77 (1968): 3–24.

sider their counterparts that do involve sensations. Let us begin with a very straightforward case in which I see a red book on my desk. I understand all the words in the sentence "I see a red book" and I might very well be disposed to utter it if circumstances made it relevant and I intended to be honest. In the ordinary case, such a disposition would be causally dependent on my eyes being affected in the customary manner by a red book. Thus, if I did utter "I see a red book" I would know that what I said was true. What I now want to ask is how we may vary this case so as to get situations that are similar to it, but that involve some sort of error. Here is a partial list.

(a) I wish it had been a blue book; my defenses are down and I say "I see a blue book." I notice the slip immediately and correct myself.

(b) This is the same case as (a), except that I do not notice the slip and thus do not correct it. I may even deny that it occurred when you try to point it out to me.

(c) I have been reading a paper on the question whether "What is red cannot be green" is a necessary truth. I have seen "red" and "green" fifty times apiece, often in close proximity. Now I am tired and any occurrence of "red" brings green to mind. Because I am slightly befuddled, I bring out "I see a green book" when I look at the red book on my desk.

(d) I have been hypnotized. I am instructed thus: "The next time you see a red book on your desk after I have said 'Wake up!' you will say 'I see a yellow book.' You will be certain that you have spoken correctly and will stoutly maintain so. You will not remember this instruction at any time after coming out of hypnosis. Wake up!" I am now gently urged in the direction of my desk. Upon espying the red book, I say "I see a yellow book."

(e) Under the influence of a (non-hallucinogenic) drug, I have fallen into a state of near idiocy in which all that seems worthwhile is to report on what I currently see. However, imagination is not completely dead and so I often report (correctly) on what I do *not* see. Thus, for example, I have recently said "I see a purple cup. I do not see a pink sheet of paper. I see a piece of black slate. I see a typewriter that is not chartreuse." My eyes now light upon my red book. I begin, "I see a book that is . . . ." Now, however, I pause, for I cannot remember whether or not I have stuck in a "not". Mistakenly remembering having done so, I continue ". . . brown."

(f) This is the same case as (e) except that I do not pause over the question of whether I have uttered a negative particle. I just leave it out without noticing my mistake and as a result say "I see a book that is brown."

(g) My desk is messy and several papers cover parts of my red book. There is also a piece of yellow acetate on it, but in the general confusion I fail to notice this. I report that I see an orange book.

We can now return to the case of sensations and settle the issue about incorrigibility. The key fact is that all of these mistakes *except* (g) could be made in reports about sensations. For (g) there is no analogue; there is nothing that counts as a sensation appearing other than it is. This is a sound point that lies behind claims that sensation reports are incorrigible. However, when incorrigibilists say that all mistakes about sensations are merely verbal, they open themselves to objection. (a) and (b) are clearly verbal errors, but what about (c)–(f)? I do not say that (c)–(f) are not verbal errors; rather, the notion of verbal error does not seem so clear that we can decide the issue. This much, however, plainly must be granted to opponents of incorrigibility: (f) is really not much like (a) and (b).

There is nothing to prevent one from reserving "verbal error" for cases like (*a*) and (*b*) and insisting on a different term (or terms) for (*c*)–(*f*). However, opponents of incorrigibility must in their turn recognize that there is at least as sharp a difference between (*a*)–(*f*), on the one side, and (*g*) on the other.

There is another way of approaching incorrigibilism that we must explore before we can leave this topic.[6] It can seem to be impossible sincerely to assert a falsehood about our sensations in words that we really understand. For correct application in standard cases is part of what is required for understanding a word; and since sensations cannot appear other than they are, all cases of having them occur in "standard conditions". Mistake, however, requires false belief and belief requires understanding. Thus, if one cannot both understand a term and misapply it to a sensation, false belief, that is, mistake about sensations, is impossible.

There is something right about this argument and also something wrong with it. The mistake is this. In order to understand a word it is *not* required that one always apply it correctly in standard cases, but only that one generally do so. To put the same point in a different guise, it trivializes an incorrigibility claim if one says that people who misclassify a sensation *must* not have understood what they were saying, even if their lack of understanding lasts only for a moment. What is right about the argument is that sensations always occur in "standard conditions"—that is, for example, there is no such thing as having them from a bad angle or through a distorting medium or from too great a distance. This corresponds to the exclusion of an analogue of (*g*) in the case of sensations. Momentary nonunderstanding of one's words does not follow from the possibility of misclassifying sensations even if we add the premise that there is no analogue of (*g*); for there are possible analogues for all of (*a*)–(*f*).

6. Cf. Chandler, "Incorrigibility and Classification".

The Given

Sensations have often been said to be *given*. Part of what is intended by this is that we have incorrigible knowledge of our sensations. The metaphor of givenness is, however, richly connected with other views. Among these are cultural relativism and the view that our knowledge must rest on a specially secure foundation. It would not be feasible to try to settle here all the issues that these views bring to mind. However, we have developed a background that will enable us profitably to consider the places where reference to sensations is particularly relevant to these views. The following remarks will show what progress we can make within this limited area.

The metaphor of givenness contains two important suggestions. The first of these, in very rough form, is the idea that *what* is given depends only on the givers, who are distinct from the recipients. The other suggestion is that what *has been* given has also to *have been* received. I shall spell out these metaphors in the following paragraphs. It will also be necessary to explore the connection between givenness and non-inferential knowledge.

We may begin by attempting to apply the first part of the metaphor of givenness to sensations. The result is the idea that what sensations (gifts) people receive depends on what affects them and not on the recipients themselves. This result cannot, of course, be accepted as it stands; for the having of sensations does depend on their "recipients" having properly working sense organs and neurons. For example, if one is anesthetized one will not get pains from things that usually cause them; and we can be color blind, tone deaf, or congenitally insensitive in various other ways. As the metaphor of givenness is customarily applied, however, all that is required is that what is to count as given is not affected by certain aspects of recipients. The relevant aspects are people's conceptual schemes and beliefs. That is, for something to count as given people must receive the same givens even if they differ in beliefs or in conceptual schemes. This formulation is still too crude, however. To motivate one of the distinctions we will need we may consider the following.

Sensations are caused by neural firings and they will therefore be the same in different people (or the same people at different times) if the same neural causes are present.[7] Further, while different causes can sometimes produce the same effect, we should generally expect that changes in the neural causes of sensations will produce changes in the sensations. We may further assume that there is some neural difference between people who hold different beliefs or who have different conceptual schemes, and also some neural difference in the states of a person who has one set of beliefs or one conceptual scheme at one time and a different set of beliefs or a different conceptual scheme at another time. These neural differences may be expected to propagate and to cause other changes in the state of a person's brain. Now, one question we can ask about givenness of sensations is the question whether the neural differences that go with differences of belief or conceptual scheme cause differences in the neural states that cause sensations.

This question is an empirical question upon which we have little direct evidence. I shall, therefore, not try to answer it. There are, however, some philosophical, non-empirical arguments about givenness that I do want to evalute. The clearest way to do this will

---

7. "Same neural causes" means, of course, "same causally relevant neural features". Thus, for example, it may be that what is relevant to my having a certain kind of pain is having some neurons firing in a certain sequence of ratios of intensity. If so, it would not be required that this sequence always take place in the firings of the same neurons, when I have the same kind of pain on different occasions. Similarly, assuming we have really identified the causally relevant features, we could attribute the same kind of pain to other people if they had the same sequence of intensity ratios, without having to suppose that there is a way of exactly mapping their neural networks onto mine in such a way as to identify unique correlates to my neurons.

be to introduce a definition and an hypothesis. The definition provides one sense of "given":

(G1)   Xs are given to people if and only if neural differences
        that can be correlated with differences in beliefs or
        conceptual schemes do not have significant direct
        effects on those neural states that cause Xs.

The "indirect" effects that are to be contrasted with the "direct" effects in (G1) are those that involve actions. For example, I might come to believe that rabbits are good to eat. Suppose this caused me to come to be on the lookout for rabbits. Then I might have more rabbit-shaped sensations than I used to have; but this would involve my actions of searching for rabbits and thus would be an indirect effect. Contrast with this the possibility that the neural changes involved in my coming to believe that rabbits would be good to eat cause changes in my visual cortex, which in turn cause me to have rabbit-shaped sensations the next time I look at a cat. This would be a direct effect in the sense intended in (G1). We will see a further suggestion about what a direct effect might look like in the next section.

I shall next introduce a Causal Independence Hypothesis:

(CIH)   Sensations are given in the sense of (G1).

Since we cannot establish to what degree (CIH) approximates reality, the best we can do is to be explicit about where we need to assume it. The further conclusions of the present section will depend on (CIH) being at least nearly correct. In the next section, I shall consider some arguments against it.

In our discussion of incorrigibility we saw that it would be possible to have a sensation of a certain kind and not to know that one had that kind of sensation. We can extend this point and say that even if sensations are given, knowledge of sensations is not given in the sense of (G1). To illustrate this point, let us imagine a group of speakers who have a word, say "grellow", that they apply to all the things that we call either "green" or "yellow" and to nothing else. We are to assume, further, that they have no word whose application coincides with our "green" or with our "yellow". To know that something is grellow is not the same as knowing it is green, nor is it the same as knowing it is yellow. Suppose we take some of these speakers and irradiate them with a bright blue light. Then, assuming (CIH), they will have yellow afterimages. They would not, however, know that they had yellow afterimages; they would know only that they had grellow ones.

It may be objected that such people might know that their afterimages are yellow if, for example, they can tell you that their afterimages have a color just like that of sulphur. This observation is correct and shows that one need not have a word for a kind of sensation that one knows one has. However, it is *possible* for a person to be able to understand "grellow" but have neither the concept of yellow nor any way of dividing off the yellow things that are grellow from the green ones. That this situation really is possible will be obvious if we consider finer differences between shades— something on the order of adjacent shades in a paint company's sample book. If you choose the right source of illumination, perhaps you can produce an afterimage in me whose color I could not distinguish from that of the sample for "antique mint". But if the sample is not before me at the time, I will not know what to call the shade of afterimage I am having and I will not be able to think of an object for comparison that has exactly that shade. I will thus know that my afterimage is pale green, but not that it is antique mint as opposed to, say, frosted lime.

We can distinguish (G1) from two other senses in which something might be given. The first of these is

(G2)   Xs are given to people if and only if their having Xs is logically independent of what conceptual scheme they possess.

The next sense of "given" depends on the following distinction. We may consider (a) beliefs that are so central to a conceptual scheme that no one who did not accept them could be using the concepts of that scheme. Let us call these "framework beliefs". In contrast we may consider (b) beliefs that could be held by some people and not held by others who use the same concepts. Let us call these "non-framework beliefs". If we say that being given should involve being logically independent of framework beliefs, we are merely giving an alternative expression of (G2). Saying the analogous thing with respect to non-framework beliefs, however, yields a distinct sense of "given".

(G3) Xs are given to people if and only if their having Xs is logically independent of what non-framework beliefs they hold.

I said above that the metaphor of givenness contained a second suggestion, to the effect that what has been given has to have been received. One might object that one can buy a gift that one has not yet given; but, of course, one can really only buy something that is intended to become a gift and that actually becomes so only upon being given to—and, therefore, received by—its recipient. This is the part of the givenness metaphor that is bound up with incorrigibility and with the appearance-reality distinction. If a sensation is "already received" then there is no further process involved in "getting" it and thus no place for something to go wrong. Realities may falsely appear, that is, cause a misleading appearance to be received; but appearances, being already received, do not cause further appearances and hence do not cause any misleading ones. To know realities I have to possess concepts, and I must also assume or show that my senses are not misleading me. To know appearances I must also possess concepts; but beyond that I need only receive them and need not make either assumptions or arguments. We can introduce a sense of "given" that corresponds to these remarks in the following way.

(G4)   Xs are given to people if and only if Xs are logically independent of anything that could falsely appear.

If we combine (G3) and (G4) we can understand the temptation to say that sensations are the foundation of knowledge. First, evidence is supposed to convince. Thus, it ought not to be question-begging; and so it ought to be independent of what one or another party to a dispute may believe. If (CIH) is true, sensations satisfy this requirement. Second, evidence ought to be reliable. The immunity of sensations to false appearance thus recommends them once again as good evidence. Finally, sensations seem to be the only things we can know about that come with such good credentials for being taken as evidence.

Let us call "foundationalism" the view that truths about what sensations we have had are the only non-logical premises that justify our knowledge and that are not in turn derived by some argument from other non-logical premises. To argue for or against this view in its own right would take us far beyond the scope of this chapter. We may, however, observe that foundationalism does not follow from the givenness of sensations. We can allow that knowledge of sensations is available for supporting other kinds of knowledge and even that it is actually so used without committing ourselves to the view that such knowledge is the only kind that is not derived by an argument.

These remarks about the foundations of knowledge may be challenged by an argument that can be derived from the writings of Wilfrid Sellars.[8] This argument occurs as part of a larger, very com-

8. See Wilfrid Sellars, "Empiricism and the Philosophy of Mind", in his *Science, Perception and Reality.*

plex argument but we may pry it loose and give it a rather simple statement. It takes the form of a dilemma. Either the given is a bit of knowledge that something is the case, or it is not. If it is, it cannot really be "given"—that is, the first horn of the dilemma is self-contradictory. The reason is that knowledge requires bringing things under concepts and concepts must be acquired. However, if the given is not a bit of knowledge that something is the case, then it cannot function as a premise in an argument. It could not be evidence for the truth of any proposition. Thus, it could not be something on which knowledge of what is not given is based.

This dilemma calls not so much for a reply as for clarification. We can get at the key point by making the following distinction. Consider a sensation report of the form "A sensation of kind *K* occurs at *t*." This report is *about* a sensation. Although I shall assume that I know that the report is true, the report is *not about* my knowledge. (What *would* be about my knowledge is, for example, "It is known by me that this report is true.") On the other hand, the report could be said to *display* my knowledge. It conveys the content of a piece of knowledge that I have. It does not display a sensation. The sensation is of some kind or other, which the report denotes by an adjective; but it has no "content" that would be properly conveyed by a sentence.

We need to note one further feature of reports of the form just introduced: if they are known at all, they are known to someone without inference. Let us call such reports "non-inferential reports". We can then introduce two further senses of "given".

(G5)   *X*s are given to people if and only if *X*s are what non-inferential reports are about.

(G6)   *X*s are given to people if and only if *X*s are what non-inferential reports display.

We can now collect our results and draw some conclusions. We have adopted the hypothesis that sensations are given in the sense of (G1).

It should be obvious that sensations are also given in the sense of (G2)–(G5), but not in the sense of (G6). On the other hand, pieces of knowledge about one's sensations are not given in the sense of (G1) or (G2). Since knowledge of sensations does not logically depend on anything except sensations and the possession of concepts, and since sensations are given in the sense of (G3), pieces of knowledge about sensations are given in the sense of (G3). They are also given in the sense of (G4) and (G6). Whether pieces of knowledge about sensations are given in the sense of (G5) depends on whether or not "I know that a sensation of kind K occurs at t" is itself known inferentially. If it is, then pieces of knowledge about sensations are not given in the sense of (G5). If it is not, they are given in the sense of (G5). It is of no consequence for present purposes which of these alternatives one accepts.

We can apply these results to the question whether knowledge of sensations can legitimately be assigned its traditional role as a "given" basis of our knowledge of matters of fact. The answer is that it depends on what issue is at hand. Thus, if the issue is whether our conceptual scheme can be justified by its conformity to what is given, the failure to have the independence in (G2) would make it clearly misleading to count knowledge of sensations as "given". We may, however, be interested in more local issues, for example, the extent to which statements about physical objects can be justified by appeal to something simpler and more secure. In a context like this (G3) and (G4) are important enough, and share enough with traditional assumptions about the given, to support a decision to count knowledge of sensations as "given".

Sensations and Conceptual Change

We have been arguing on the hypothesis that sensations are causally independent of conceptual schemes. I have remarked that we do not have direct, that is, neurophysiological evidence for or against this hypothesis. There are, however, some philosophical arguments that might be thought to cast doubt on it. In this section, I shall consider two such arguments.

The first argument derives from Thomas Kuhn. I say "derives" because I do not think Kuhn means to be taken as strongly as he would have to be taken if he were attacking (CIH). Nonetheless, he does suggest that Galileo's experience of swinging stones was different from Aristotle's. He suggests that the former would have seen pendulums where the latter would have seen constrained falling bodies.[9] Since this is put in terms of seeing, someone might suppose that a difference of (visual) sensations must be involved. It might then be thought natural to claim that the difference between the Galilean and Aristotelian conceptual schemes is the cause of the difference in sensations; and thus (CIH) might be thought to be falsified.

It is easy to reply to such an argument; indeed, the reply can be fashioned from Kuhn's own words. Surely, Galileo and Aristotle were both able to see *swinging stones*. It is most implausible to suppose that either of them lost the ability to see swinging stones— and to see them *as* swinging stones—just by coming to accept his particular brand of physics.

In this case, we actually have three conceptual schemes: one involving the concept of constrained fall; one involving the concept of a pendulum; and one involving the concept of swinging stones. I have argued, in effect, that possessing either of the first two does not debar us from possessing the third. If this is right, we may not only suppose that Galileo and Aristotle could have had the same kind of sensation when looking at swinging stones but also that they could have understood a common description, namely "looking like

9. See Thomas Kuhn, *The Structure of Scientific Revolutions* (2nd ed.; Chicago: University of Chicago Press, 1970), pp. 121, 123, and 128.

swinging stones". However, having such a common description does not seem to be necessary for having the same sensation type. If our remarks about Aristotle and Galileo are correct, then acquiring the concept of a pendulum does not change one's sensation. We could put this by saying that when one looks at a pendulum, one can have the same sensation that one has when one looks at a swinging stone. If this is so, however, there seems to be no reason why a community could not retain their same pendulum sensations even if they were to abandon the concept (and the description) "swinging stones". Thus we can envisage the possibility of two groups beginning by sharing sensations and descriptions but developing in such a way that, in the fullness of time, they would still have the same sensation kinds, but no longer any common terms to apply to them.

I turn now to an argument that has been offered by Paul Churchland and that is explicitly concerned with sensations and conceptual change. I should perhaps remark that Churchland is also concerned to clarify the possibilities just described and that many of his arguments are concerned with showing knowledge of sensations not to be given in the sense of (G2). The following quotation, however, goes beyond this point. It comes from his book *Scientific Realism and the Plasticity of Mind*.[10] It comes immediately after a discussion of cases where we have "a mere reconception of states already introspected under some familiar conception or other." Churchland continues, "There appears to be a great deal about our physiological and neurological activities—activities currently opaque to us— that we can *come to* recognize introspectively, given the concepts with which to classify them and the training necessary to apply those concepts reliably in non-inferential judgments." In his book,

10. Paul Churchland, *Scientific Realism and the Plasticity of Mind* (Cambridge: Cambridge University Press, 1979). The two quotations that follow both appear on p. 119.

Churchland just throws this out and passes on immediately to another point. In a subsequent paper, however, he has developed it at some length.[11] At the climax of this paper, he speaks of "the changes in our introspective apprehension of our internal states that could follow upon a wholesale revision in our conceptual framework for our internal states" (25). He further says, "[S]uppose that Mary has learned to conceptualize her inner life, even in introspection, in terms of the completed neuroscience we are to imagine. So she does *not* identify her visual sensations crudely as "a sensation of black" . . . ; *rather* she identifies them more revealingly as various spiking frequencies . . . " (25–26; emphasis mine.)

Churchland's argument for being willing to speak in these ways begins with the fact that musicians, wine tasters, and others can learn to respond to the presence of distinct components in what to the untutored is a single, undifferentiated sensation.[12] As one learns about musical structure, one learns how to hear which notes compose a chord; as one learns about wines, one learns how to taste the glycol and the tannin; and so on. The conclusion to which these facts seem to point is that what kinds of sensations one can have is changeable and that acquiring new concepts with which to describe one's sensations can lead to the ability to have the corresponding sensations.

There are two points to be made against drawing this conclusion.

---

11. See Paul Churchland, "Reduction, Qualia, and the Direct Introspection of Brain States", *Journal of Philosophy* 82 (1985): 8–28. Parenthetical numbers in the remainder of this section refer to pages of this article.

12. Churchland's format involves proposing a scheme for neurophysiological reduction and rebutting arguments that such a reduction must fail. I am distilling out only what seem to me to be the positive considerations for advancing the quoted views. I am interested here only in those points that seem to cut against (CIH); I am making no comment on the arguments concerned solely with the reducibility of sensations.

The first is that we must not put *training* and *concept acquisition* together as if they were not relevantly different in this context. Training, of the sort involved in music and oenology, involves the stimulation of the sense organs. We would naturally expect this to produce effects in sensory neurons and hence effects in synapses that these neurons have on other neurons. Since sensations are often produced by stimulation of sense organs, we would naturally expect neural changes of the kind described to lead to new possibilities of sensations. This sort of change, however, does not lead to conflict with (CIH). That is, it is not a case of *conceptual* change alone leading to change in sensations. Instead, it is a case where both the conceptual change and the change in sensations are effects of repeated stimulation of sense organs.

The second point is this. We can (at least in principle) get some purified (although diluted) tannin or glycol and put it on the tongue of a naive taster. In this case we would not expect the naiveté to be any bar to tasting the chemical. Analogously, we could play a single note instead of a chord; this would be heard even by the musically uneducated. So what Churchland's cases show is not even that training can cause us to have a sensation that we could not have had before training. Instead they show that training is necessary to come to have certain sensations under certain circumstances, that is, circumstances where causes of several sensations of the same sense modality are present. This observation should help make it clear that it is not concept acquisition as such that makes a sensation available, but rather the training in discrimination that makes articulated combinations of sensations available. Thus, once again, (CIH) is not undercut.

Toward the end of his paper, Churchland introduces material that appears to contain a way around both of the points just made. This part of his argument depends on a certain analogy between sight and music and I shall begin by sketching it. Recent work on vision shows that the color of an object is determined by reflectance efficiencies at three wavelengths.[13] It is plausible that this triune structure is preserved in our visual systems. So it is plausible that the colors of our sensations are determined by triples of activity coefficients in some parts of our visual systems. The analogy with music is that chords are composed of triples (or quadruples etc.) of tones. Now, musicians can learn to hear chords as composed of their several tones. They can write down what individual tones were sounded upon hearing them presented together in a chord. So it seems natural that someone who attended in the right way to color sensations might come to appreciate them as triples of some kind.

Two further points need to be introduced in order to see how this analogy is to be used. First, Churchland imagines "a brilliant neuroscientist named Mary, who has lived her entire life in a room that is rigorously controlled to display only various shades of black, white, and grey" (22). She knows all about the physical structure of neural events in the visual system and the rest of the brain. Churchland supposes that Mary may acquire the concepts of the neurophysiological states corresponding to color sensations by her study of the brain and be enabled by this alone to imagine sensations she has not yet had (26). He suggests that we might, at last, allow her to see a ripe tomato and that she might, "*on introspective grounds alone*", identify the resulting sensation as "a spiking frequency of 90 hz in the gamma network" (26). The analogy with music is invoked by Churchland in order to support the view that such a precocious introspector is possible.

The last point we need here is that Churchland suggests that Mary's introspective ability depends on being "informed" or "conceptually sophisticated" (27). If we put this together with the foregoing, we get the view that increase in *conceptual* sophistication might make us able to have our sensations take on a complexity that

13. Churchland, whom I follow here, bases his account on the work of Edwin Land. He refers to Land's "The Retinex Theory of Color Vision", *Scientific American* 237 (1977): 108–128.

is not entirely due to training. Moreover, this would not be a case of recognizing, in a complex presentation, elements that could have been presented singly to the conceptually unsophisticated; it would involve having a completely new sensation element. Now, if all this could be made out, we would have a case where a conceptual development would account for a difference in what sensation kinds are available to us, over and above any difference that could be put down to training. Thus, we would have a reason to reject (CIH).

Churchland's case, cannot, however, be made out. The problem lies in the supposed analogy between color vision and music. This analogy is intended to make it plausible that some of our neural activities might come to appear to us *as* having triples of neural properties. But if we spell out the analogy in question, it will be clear that we have no reason at all to expect such a result. To see that this is so, consider what would be the color vision analogy to the hearing of a single tone. It would be the seeing of an object under illumination by monochromatic light at one of the three crucial wavelengths. The analogue of learning to predict a chordal sound from three notes given singly would be learning to predict how a thing would look in ordinary daylight from successive monochromatic illuminations of it at each of the three crucial wavelengths. The analogue of learning to tell what notes compose a sound given as a chord would be learning to say what an object viewed in daylight would look like under each of the monochromatic illuminations. Now, all this is just like the case of wine tasting that we considered above. For example, those who know nothing about neurophysiology can be expected to see an object under monochromatic illumination. There is no more reason to expect such exposure to make our color sensations appear to us as neurologically complex than there is to expect the tasting of purified chemicals to make our tastes appear to us as neurologically complex, or, for that matter, the hearing of single tones to make our auditory sensations appear to us as neurologically complex. I conclude, therefore, that the only genuine phenomenon that Churchland mentions is our ability to come to have recognizably complex sensations when we are presented with several causes of sensations of the same modality at the same time. This, however, can be put down to neural development resulting from training. We thus have found no reason to think that concept acquisition *per se* is a cause of change in our sensations; that is, we have found no reason to abandon (CIH).

CHAPTER III

Thinking

One of the oldest distinctions in philosophy is the distinction between the senses, on the one hand, and reason or intellect on the other. In the present chapter, we will turn to the second half of this distinction. Our guiding question will be whether a consideration of our ability to think requires us to suppose that there is something non-physical about us. First, however, we must give explicit and careful formulation to the ancient sense/reason distinction.

Thinking versus Sensations

What Thinkings Are

For reasons that will become apparent later on, I shall use the term "thinking" in a special way. Partially following Descartes, I shall use "thinking" as a generic term, whose species are believing, doubting, desiring, wondering, hoping, and so on.[1] More startlingly, I shall use "thinking" and the names of its species with divided reference.

---

1. Of course, unlike Descartes, I am *excluding* sensations from the scope of the term "thinking". I shall also generally avoid one ordinary use of "thinking", although it could be included as a species under my term. This is thinking about a problem, or *pondering*. A case of pondering is complex, typically involving many cases of believing, concluding, wondering, and so on.

Thus, I shall speak of a case in which someone believes something as *a believing,* a case in which someone desires something as *a desiring,* and so on. All of these will be thinkings.

To fully understand and justify our use of "(a) thinking" we need to know what distinguishes one thinking from another. The required method of individuation can be given as follows. No thinking can be of more than one species; thus any believing (for example) is different from any desiring. Further, a thinking can be the thinking of only one person; thus, if x and y are thinkings of different people, that is sufficient to show that they are different thinkings. Finally, each thinking is characterized by some sentence that can be used to report it. For example, every case of believing is a case of believing that such and such is the case and some sentence can be used to say what is believed. Again, every case of desiring is a case of desiring that such and such be the case and some sentence can be used to say what it is that is desired.[2] Sentences can be used to express what is hoped for, wondered about, and so on. Now, thinkings are individuated by the rule that non-synonymous sentences characterize different thinkings.

These remarks will explain what counts as one case of thinking in most contexts. However, we need something more if the sentence used to specify a thinking refers to a current condition without dating it. In such cases, the difference of time at which thinkings occur distinguishes them. Thus, if Jones now believes it is raining, that is a different believing from his believing last week that it was then raining, even though what we would have said last week in answer to "What does Jones believe?" is "It is raining." However, difference of time does not distinguish believings in the case of standing sentences. If Jones has believed for forty years that the Earth is round, that is to count as one case of believing.[3]

2. Actually, two sentences are always available for characterizing desirings, one of which is in the indicative mood (for example, "I want some food") and one of which is a corresponding imperative (for example, "Give me some food, please").

3. One *could* subdivide thinkings into temporal units as short as you please, just as

It will be wondered why I do not use a term that already has divided reference in its customary use, namely "thoughts". The reason is that this term would carry unwanted associations. Specifically, "(a) thought" has often been used to denote a putative "inner episode" of a certain kind, where an *inner* episode means either an episode literally in the head, that is, a brain event, or an event in a hidden, mental realm. I shall be wanting to cast doubt on or deny the need for commitment to some views that recognize thoughts in this sense. Hence, I need a term that will allow me to talk of cases of people believing and desiring things without repeatedly suggesting the very views that I mean to argue are false or not evident. This is the role assigned to "thinkings".

Intentionality

We must now introduce a second technical term, "intentionality". Unlike "(a) thinking" this term is not peculiar to my own usage, but has been introduced by many philosophers.[4] There are two ways, in

---

one *could* subdivide chairs into 5-nanosecond chair-stages. There will be no reason to do this here. The only reason we shall divide believings of standing sentences is if there is a double change of belief. For example, if Jones gets brainwashed by Flat Earthers but then gets deprogrammed so that he *once again* believes that the Earth is round, I shall say that there have been two cases of Jones' believing that the Earth is round.

4. There are many discussions of intentionality. Among the best are those of Gustav Bergmann, "Intentionality", in Bergmann, *Meaning and Existence* (Madison: University of Wisconsin Press, 1960); Roderick Chisholm, *Perceiving: A Philosophical Study* (Ithaca, N.Y.: Cornell University Press, 1957), chap. 11; D. C. Dennett, *Content and Consciousness* (New York: Humanities Press, 1969). chap. 2, and "Intentional Systems", in Dennett, *Brainstorms* (Bradford Books, 1978); Wilfrid Sellars, "Empiricism and the Philosophy of Mind" and "Some Reflections on Language Games", in Sellars, *Science, Perception and Reality* (London: Routledge & Kegan Paul, 1963); and the correspondence between Sellars and Chisholm in Herbert Feigl *et al.*, eds., *Concepts, Theories, and the Mind-Body Problem, Minnesota Studies in the Philosophy of Science*, vol. 2 (Minneapolis: University of Minnesota Press, 1958), pp. 521–539.

fact, in which "intentionality" is commonly introduced. One of these associates intentionality with *being about, meaning, being directed upon, standing for,* or *denoting*. Whatever is about, means, and so on is said to *have* intentionality. Thus, words and sentences have intentionality, because they mean something, stand for something, and are about things. Thoughts, in the technical sense of inner episodes, are held to have intentionality by those who talk about them at all; in fact, we can take it as a definition of a *thought* that it is an inner episode that has intentionality. Thinkings also have intentionality. Believings, for example, are always believings about something; desirings and hopings are always directed upon the coming to be of some state of affairs.

What can be said to have intentionality can also be said to be intentional. Here, however, we must be careful. Having intentionality in general (and thus also, being intentional, in general) has nothing specially to do with being done as the result of an intention to bring something about. In *some* cases intentions are present in a case of intentionality. Thus, typical cases of actions are intentional (in the sense of having intentionality) because they are directed upon (the bringing about of) some result; and they are *also* intentional in the sense of being done with an intention, that is, being done intentionally rather than accidentally, inadvertently, or by mistake. But in other cases, for example, cases of believings, there is intentionality (that is, aboutness) without intentions to do anything. In what follows we shall be interested exclusively in having intentionality, and any occurrence of "(to be) intentional" is to be taken in the sense of "(to have) intentionality".

The second way in which "intentionality" is often introduced connects it with a peculiarity that shows up in certain arguments. We can focus on the relevant feature by considering the two following cases. First, there is the straightforward and valid argument,

Jones uses his paring knife to open his letters.
Jones' paring knife is (identical with) the weapon that killed

Smith. Therefore,
Jones uses the weapon that killed Smith to open his letters.

Second, there is the largely similar argument,

Jones believes his paring knife is on his desk.
Jones' paring knife is (identical with) the weapon that killed
Smith. Therefore,
Jones believes the weapon that killed Smith is on his desk.

In contrast to the first argument, this one is not valid; we may well imagine that while the premises are true, Jones would be quite horrified to learn that he was making casual use of the very weapon that skewered his dear friend Smith. What is peculiar about the argument is that the conclusion is derived from the first premise by making a substitution, which the second premise tells us is a substitution of words that refer to the very same thing. This is all that we did in the (valid) first argument. Clearly, substitution of identicals is *in general* legitimate. According to the second way of introducing "intentionality," *contexts* in which substitution of identicals does not yield valid conclusions are called "intentional contexts". Next, it is noted that the use of certain verbs, for example, "believes", "desires", "wonders whether", and "fears" produces intentional contexts. Such verbs are called "intentional verbs". Finally, states described by the use of intentional verbs, for example, believing something or desiring something, are said to have intentionality.[5]

In what follows, I shall take the first way of introducing "intentionality" to be fundamental. This permits us to ask why it is that reports about what has intentionality (in the sense of the first introduction) should exhibit the peculiarity that gives rise to the second introduction. We shall be in a position to say something enlightening about this later on.

5. A detailed version of the second way of introducing intentionality can be found in Chisholm, *Perceiving,* chap. 11.

We can now return to the distinction between sense and reason. The revision I want to make is to recast this as the distinction between thinkings and sensations. We have already seen that thinkings have intentionality. I now add that sensations do not have intentionality. Naturally, *believings* about pains or believings about the causes of pains have intentionality and so do desirings to be rid of pains. But the pains themselves are not about anything, directed upon anything, nor do they stand for, mean, or denote anything. Thus, one basis on which the distinction between thinkings and sensations can be made is that thinkings are intentional while sensations are not.

Qualia

The term "qualia" (singular, "quale") has had some currency as a way of indicating the qualities of sensations. I shall, in fact, define "qualia" as "non-relational qualities that sensations can have". Given this definition it is, of course, trivial to say that sensations have qualia. However, it is not trivial that, as we have seen in Chapter I, sensations have color qualities, pitch qualities, timbres, flavors, savors, and so on, or that they literally resemble and differ in the corresponding respects.

By contrast, thinkings do not have qualia. What thinkings are about may have them. I can, for example, wonder whether there is any blue food or desire that my walls be painted white. This evidently does not make my wondering blue or my desire white. Nor do thinkings have qualia like pain or itchiness. Believings about, say, the causes of itches differ from believings about the causes of pains; but one who investigates the causes of itches cannot be expected to suffer more itching than the rest of us. Again, some thinkings may cause feelings, as my believing that Mary is with John may cause jealousy; but a different believing could have caused the same feeling (had I loved Ann rather than Mary) and the same believing could have caused a different feeling (had I never loved Mary). Thus, the feeling quality that may occur together with a believing cannot be held to be a quality of the believing itself. Finally, there are feelings that go with desiring things and perhaps there is a feeling that always comes with desiring and so could be called "the feeling of desire". However, different desires are directed upon different states of affairs and so must contain something that differs from one case to another. This gives us a reason for regarding any feeling that may accompany desiring as at best a *part* of a desiring; that is, it enables us to distinguish what has a quale from whatever it is about a desiring that has to do with its being directed upon this rather than that state of affairs.

We now have two ways of making the distinction between thinkings and sensations; one and only one has intentionality and the other alone has qualia. There are, of course, also some similarities. For example, both thinkings and sensations have appeared to require that there be something non-physical about us and both seem to be the kinds of things about which we can have certainty. These similarities have given rise to the concept of *mind,* which embraces both thinkings and sensations. Many philosophers, among them recent functionalists, have attempted to give unified treatments of mental states, that is, single accounts designed to cover both thinkings and sensations. However, the differences we have just remarked are fundamental. They make a parallel treatment of thinkings and sensations the very last thing we should expect. Indeed, we are about to see that the right way of looking at thinkings and intentionality is quite different from what we have seen to be required for sensations.

An Account of Intentionality

I have just alluded to the fact that thinkings have seemed to require that there is something non-physical about human beings. We shall eventually examine this appearance from several angles. We may begin, however, with a view associated with the name of Franz Brentano. According to Brentano, intentionality always presupposes the presence of something psychological and is never present when we are dealing with purely physical phenomena.[6] It follows that if what human beings say or do has intentionality, they are not purely physical phenomena. Roderick Chisholm has given this thesis a linguistic turn.[7] He has argued that the peculiarity that characterizes intentional contexts (see above) never shows up when we describe purely physical phenomena, but that when we describe psychological phenomena we cannot avoid it, except by specially contrived terms that we never need when describing the purely physical. Once again, the implication is that, in so far as we exhibit psychological phenomena, we are not purely physical.

The question that will be under discussion for some time is whether intentionality does in fact provide a good reason to believe that there is something about us that is non-physical. My contention will be that it does not. I cannot quite say that my account will mention nothing at all that is non-physical. But when it does so, it will be clear that whatever contribution the non-physical makes is parasitic on a grounding of intentionality that does not appeal to anything non-physical.

One of the views that I will be opposing locates intentionality primarily in a non-physical thought or (*mental*) *act*. There are, however, accounts that are alternatives to mine, but that are still physicalistic. Like the mental act view, these accounts locate intentionality primarily in *thoughts*. Unlike the mental act view, however, they hold thoughts to be physical. In contrast to both views, I shall locate intentionality—roughly speaking—primarily in behavior. It is natural to ask what is wrong with the views that I shall reject. It is, however, often possible to see where the arguments for these

6. See Franz Brentano, *Psychology from the Empirical Standpoint,* ed. Oskar Kraus, tr. A. C. Rancurello *et al.* (New York: Humanities Press, 1973), pp. 88–89.
7. See Chisholm, *Perceiving,* chap. 11.

views fail only when one has some clear idea of a possible alternative view. Accordingly, I shall begin by presenting my own account of intentionality.

Behavior, Believings, and Desirings

It is a truism that what people do is indicative of what they believe and what they want. It is not truistic, however, to say that what people do and what they would do in this or that circumstance is *constitutive* of their thinkings. This substantive claim is the core of *behaviorism*. It would be saying too much to articulate behaviorism as the claim that the evidence about people's behavior and dispositions to behave settles every question that might be raised about their thinkings; for some questions may be in principle irresolvable. But we can articulate behaviorism as the view that if we knew everything there was to know about people's behavior and dispositions to behave, we would know everything required to settle any question about thinkings that can be settled at all. In this remark, as in all that follows, "behavior" is to be understood to include linguistic behavior. It will be convenient to have a term for non-linguistic behavior: bearing in mind the adage that actions speak louder than words, I shall use "action" for this purpose. To forestall possible misunderstanding, I should say that linguistic utterances are, of course, actions in one ordinary sense of the term; for example, they are things for which we may be held responsible.

The view I shall present is a species of behaviorism. This remark will immediately prompt some to raise a critical question that has been considered to pose an unsolvable problem for at least some forms of behaviorism. I shall begin by rehearsing this objection, for the reply to it will bring out some central features of the view I intend to propose.[8]

8. This problem was raised by R. Chisholm, *ibid.*, by Peter Geach in *Mental Acts* (London: Routledge & Kegan Paul, 1957), pp. 8–9, and by many others since.

The problem that proponents of behaviorism must face is that no particular behavior is required of one who has this or that thinking. For example, consider people who believe that a bear is wandering about uncaged in their vicinity. This may lead them to remove themselves, but only if they also desire safety and believe they have no power to control the bear. Those who believe they are bear trainers, or believe that bears can be transfixed by a steady stare, and those who desire a speedy and spectacular death may not leave the vicinity, but may approach the bear or even try to raise its ire. Again, those who are hungry may eat good food, but they may not do so if they believe the food to be poisoned or consecrated. These examples show that one thinking does not lead to a bit of behavior; at best a whole set of thinkings does so. Looking at the same point from the side of behavior we can see also that no bit of behavior requires any particular thinking, or even any whole set of thinkings. For example, people who drink a glass of beer may believe it's beer and desire to slake their thirst; or they may not be thirsty at all but only trying to commit suicide in the (false) belief that what they are drinking is nitric acid; or they may believe (truly or falsely) that their drinking is part of a sacred rite; or they may not be thirsty but believe that beer will cure some ailment they have; and so on, and so on. We can sum up the point of these examples in the charge that behavior cannot determine thinkings, since no behavior is either necessary or sufficient for any thinking. Further, if we try to add something to behavior to connect it with thinkings, what we must add is other thinkings. This makes the project of behaviorism—that is, the exhibiting of behavior and dispositions toward behavior as determinative of thinkings—appear circular. I shall let this appearance give a name to the problem I have been outlining: I shall refer to it as the circularity problem.

The circularity problem will be with us a long time. The first step toward solving it is to relocate it as a problem about what people say. To do this we will need to make some preliminary points about thinkings. We can introduce these points by considering the following claim about the Truth of Thinking-Attributions.

(TTA) Let T be an attribution of some thinking to S, where the thinking can be characterized by "p".
Then T is true just in case S behaves like a person who *says* "p".

The obvious objection that will be raised against this is that it presupposes that there is something that counts as behaving like a person who says "p". Indeed, one might simply rephrase a point already made and assert that there is nothing that a person who says "p" has to do. This is, of course, correct. Nonetheless, in the next section I shall explain and defend the view that, after all, there is such a thing as behaving like a person who says "p". For the moment I wish to assume that I can make good on this and show what progress, small though it is, this assumption now allows us.

We can express our version of behaviorism a little more formally in the following way.

(B) For each thinking-attribution T there is some way of behaving W such that T holds of a subject S just in case S behaves in the way W.

If we try to specify W in terms of single actions, like running away or drinking, we cannot get substituends that make (B) true. If we limit ourselves to such action descriptions and try to add things to make (B) true, we fall into circularity because what we have to add are further thinkings. But (B) does not rule out a different kind of specification of W; and (TTA) provides a specification of a subject's behavior that (as we shall see) makes (B) true and does not require additions.

These remarks may prompt the following question. How could there be any use in being told what people's thinkings are, if all we are really told is that they behave like p-sayers and we are not given any description of what it is to behave like this? To answer this we must first think of cases in which we are present when people say things. Others' words have effects on us, of which we may usefully distinguish four kinds. First, people may express what they want. For example, they may say "Please turn the heat up." This may induce us to act, either to satisfy or to frustrate their want. Expression of a believing may prompt us to immediate behavior, for example, our own expression of a contrary view. Or someone's declaration that she has just seen a professional pickpocket leave the room may lead us to check our pockets. In a second kind of case, our response may be delayed. For example, a candidate's statements may get our vote, but we cannot actually cast it until election day. In a third kind of case, our response may be not only delayed but contingent upon some further behavior of the speaker. For example, I may be given to understand that my friend wishes to meet eligible women. This may produce nothing noticeable; but when, on a later occasion, he says that he finds so and so attractive it may have its effect by being part of what leads me to make an introduction. The fourth kind of case is a species of the third; that is, it involves a certain kind of delayed response that is contingent upon a particular kind of further behavior of the speaker. The particular kind of behavior that is (definitionally) required for this kind of case is behavior that is inconsistent with earlier behavior. The required response is an accusation that someone's behavior is inconsistent. "Inconsistent" here does not, of course, mean "logically inconsistent" (although uttering logical inconsistencies is a special case of it); "inconsistent" in its ordinary use is a notion that covers a wide range of inappropriate sequences of behavior.[9]

It is natural, in this last sort of case, to speak of *expectations*. We

9. My use of inconsistency and appropriateness (of behavior) here is not question-begging, although it may appear so. Inconsistent or inappropriate behavior occurs if S says "p", or gives us reason to treat S like a p-sayer, but does not later act like a p-sayer. This *of course* presupposes that there is such a thing as behaving like a person who says "p". But, as I have said, I am *assuming* this in the present section. I shall argue for it in the next section.

must, however, be careful to note that an expectation is just a state of a person that will causally contribute to making an objection or charge of inconsistency upon some future occurrence (which, of course, will be described as "what was not expected"). In particular, we must bear in mind that expectations need not have been articulated—or even articulatable—by those who have them. We do not typically go about asserting, even to ourselves, all that we expect of others; we often discover what we have expected only by finding ourselves inclined to think that some observed behavior is inconsistent with some past performance.

Let us return to our question about what good could be done by being told what others think, when this does not describe what they will do. The key lies in noticing that the responses and expectations that we have to people's saying things in our presence can be evoked by reports of what they have said. Thus, we may adjust the thermostat (up or down) by being told that someone wants the heat turned up. We may check our pockets if someone tells us that Jones has just said that a pickpocket was here. We may vote for people on the strength of reports of what they say. If a third party tells me that my friend has said he wants to meet people, that will prompt an introduction when an appropriate occasion arises. Finally, I may find people's behavior inconsistent with what I have been told they have said. Now, reports of what people say do not describe what they will do but there should by now be no surprise in the fact that there is a point to them. What they do is to *mobilize* in us the responses and expectations that we would have had if we had actually heard the subjects of reports say what they are reported to have said. My further claim is that this is also the function of reports of what people think. These do not, of course, imply that people actually said the words in which their thinkings are reported (neither is it implied that they did not say them); but otherwise the functions of the two kinds of report are the same.

We could express this view of the function of reports of thinkings by saying that they invite hearers to treat subjects of the reports as if they had said the sentence in which the thinking is reported. To treat as if is, however, to pretend and in subsequent discussions I shall refer to the function of reports of thinkings as being to invite us to pretend that the subject of the report has said "p", where p is the sentence that characterizes the thinking that is reported. This will always mean that the function of reports of thinkings is to invite us to allow our responses and expectations to act in our lives just as if we had heard the subjects say "p" (whether or not we believe they actually said "p"). I shall draw some consequences of this view of the function of reports of thinkings below. First, however, we must return to the circularity problem and defend our presuppositions about saying and behavior.

Language and Normalcy

The circularity problem, in the form we now have to consider it, is this. (TTA) presupposes that there is such a thing as behaving like a person who has recently said "p". But, it seems, people can say "p" and go on to do anything you please. Further, people who say "p" and also say "q" may behave quite differently from those who say "p" and also say "r". These latter may in turn behave differently from those who say "r" but do not say "p". So it looks as if no saying of anything would be more closely associated with one kind of behavior than it would be with indefinitely many others and that, therefore, no behavior counts as "behaving like a person who says 'p'". We may add that these problems arise without any suggestion that sayings may be insincere. Recognizing this possibility only makes the connection between a saying and further behavior more tenuous.

The solution to this problem lies in attending to certain facts involving normal conditions. Some of these are very general and are closely connected with the conditions for our survival. For example, people who are exposed to inclement weather normally wear protective clothing or else do things that bring them closer to being sheltered. People who have not recently eaten normally do things that get food into their stomachs. People who have not slept for more than sixteen hours normally do things that bring them closer to being able to sleep. Healthy people who have not had sex for more than two weeks normally do things that increase the probability of their having sexual relations in the forseeable future.

It would be a mistake to object to these claims by pointing out that someone could stand naked in the cold as a penance, or go on a hunger strike, or play Pac Man for forty hours, or take a vow of celibacy. For the above claims state what is normally the case, not what is always the case. It would be just as mistaken to suggest that what one should really say is that the exposed normally do what they *believe* will protect or shelter them, that the hungry normally do what they *believe* will get food into their stomachs, and so on. These are normalcy claims and they are true; but they are weaker than the ones to which I want to call attention. It is normal for people *actually to succeed* in getting protected when they are exposed, in getting food into their stomachs when hungry, in getting sleep after a long day, and in doing things that increase the likelihood of having sexual relations.[10]

A second kind of normalcy claim is concerned with the Normal Effects of Utterances. I shall begin by stating it. Explanations will follow.

(NEU)   For many *p*, there is at least one circumstance *C* and an effect *E* such that

   (i)   *C* can be specified without reference to the thinkings of those who utter "*p*", and

   (ii)   normally, when people utter "*p*" in *C, E* ensues.

---

10. It follows that what people believe concerning the means of getting protected, fed, and so on is normally correct. This formulation, however, reintroduces the notion of believing and in the present context it is essential to see that we do not *need* to introduce it.

This normalcy claim is not asserted for all p because of cases like the following. There are no plausible candidates for C and E that would satisfy (NEU) if we substitute for p "The curfew tolls the knell of parting day." However, for a very large range of cases, (NEU) does hold. A few illustrations will make its point clear. (i) Standing in front of the meat counter, I say to the butcher "I'd like a pound of ground chuck." This almost always has the result that the butcher hands a pound of ground chuck over the counter. "Please pass the potatoes", said at table, if there are indeed potatoes being served, almost always is followed by the potatoes coming around in my direction. (ii) I look out the window and say, "It's raining." This will normally produce an expectation in hearers who cannot see out the window. The evidence for this claim is that if I am present when they move and can see out the window, and if they see no signs of recent rain, they will almost always say, "I thought you said it rained" or something tantamount to this, in a tone of mild indignation. (iii) I ask someone where the courthouse is. She replies, "Three blocks west and two blocks south." I would almost always start walking either west or south, counting blocks as I go. I would also have an expectation of encountering a courthouse if I go three blocks west and two south. (iv) My host says, "Martinis are best if the gin/vermouth ratio is six to one." This will cause an expectation that this is how his martinis will be mixed. People will pointedly mention what they thought he said, if he turns out to mix his martinis four to one; they will ask for a lower ratio if they like their martinis less dry. (v) A mathematician says in a lecture, "Dividing through $(a^2 - ab)$ by a, we get $a - 1$." This will almost always produce an objection from some member of the audience. (vi) A physicist is being interviewed for a job. He declares that there must be hidden variables that will yield a deterministic explanation of quantum mechanical relations. He is not hired.

A temptation may arise here that is parallel to the one that arose for our non-linguistic cases. This is to amend (NEU) so as to say that E ensues when utterers of p *believe* they are in C or are believed by others to be in C. Such an amended version would be true, but not to the point. We are not here looking for necessary and sufficient conditions for occurrences of E. The point is rather that the normalcy claim (NEU) is true, just as it stands. Again, there may be a temptation to object that (NEU) is true only *because* people *believe* certain things (that is, about circumstances or about other people) and that this fact will somehow reintroduce the circularity problem. This objection, however, both changes the subject and threatens to beg the question. It changes the subject because (NEU) is not about causes at all; it neither implies nor excludes any particular explanation of why it is true. It is not designed to lead to an argument that has a premise of the form "(NEU) is caused to be true by X" (nor to one of the form "(NEU) is *not* caused to be true by X"). I shall instead be arguing only from the *truth* of (NEU). The objection threatens to beg the question in so far as it may suggest that there cannot be an account of why (NEU) is true that does not render my whole procedure circular. In response I can say only that it is part of my project to be explicit about the relation between the philosophical account of intentionality and possible views as to the causes of intentionality. I cannot complete this project until Chapter IV. By the end of that chapter, however, there should not be even an appearance of the suggested circularity.

It may be helpful briefly to consider a particular example of the kind of objection just mentioned. Thus, it might be supposed that (NEU) is plausible only because we usually assume that other people are psychologically normal. Now, there is a response to this that I believe to be correct and that concisely summarizes the perspective I shall develop. It is that, conversely to the order suggested by the objection, we usually think people are psychologically normal because, usually, they behave normally. Moreover, what oneself or others have recently said is part of what fixes a situation as one in which certain behavior is normal. This response, of course, cannot be supposed to be evidently correct at this point. I hope it will be so, however, by the end of my argument.

Once these remarks about how (NEU) is to be taken are understood, one may wish for more than illustrations in support of it. There are two arguments that we can offer here. The first is that it is easy in very many cases to think of a C and an E to go with a given p. For many p, just hearing it makes us think of a typical situation in which someone's saying it would usually have a particular sequel. It would be hard to explain how we could have such immediate responses to many sentences unless (NEU) were true. The second argument is that it is hard to see how language could either be learned or be meaningful if (NEU) were not true. Language would not be learned if it did not do learners some good. But it cannot do learners any good unless they can anticipate the results of many of their utterances. "Anticipate", like "expect" in the present context, does not involve conscious rehearsal. Thus, I am not saying that language learners have to rehearse the consequences of their utterances before making them. Instead, I am saying that there must be whatever causes are required to account for the fact that, in general, when they bring out a certain utterance, they are not unpleasantly surprised by what ensues. Now, one of these causes is a sensitivity to features of situations in which, normally, if they say "p" a certain thing will happen. This, however, is possible only if *there are* features of situations in which, normally, if they say "p" a certain thing will happen; that is to say, only if (NEU) is satisfied. Likewise, if there were not many p for which there were some C and E that satisfied (NEU), language could not be meaningful. One has to imagine, for example, what would happen to "Please pass the potatoes" if this routinely increased the proximity of peas rather than potatoes—or if it routinely got the potatoes thrown at one's head. In such a case, "potatoes" or "pass" would not mean what they mean in English; someone who wanted the potatoes passed would either have to say something else or remain frustrated. Likewise, "Three blocks west and two blocks south" would not mean what it does if it did not generally serve as a successful guide to those who receive it as a direction. The point can be extended to all our examples and many other cases: put generally, it is that if our words did not have their usual effects under certain circumstances, they would either mean something different or they would have no meaning at all.

The solution to the circularity problem requires that there be something that counts as behaving like a person who says "*p*". It is time to ask how (NEU) will help show that there is such a thing, assuming, as I shall henceforth do, that (NEU) is true. We may begin with some imperatives. People may say "Let's eat", "Please, let me go to bed", "I want an umbrella", or "Shall we make love?" In the circumstances in which these are normally said, their normal sequels are, respectively, eating, sleeping, protection against the rain, and lovemaking. These facts give us reason to associate certain kinds of behavior with these sentences and thus reason to think of these kinds of behavior if we are told that someone behaves like a person who has uttered one of them.

On the view I am proposing, attributing desirings is the same thing as attributing patterns of behavior under descriptions of the form "behaves like one who says '*p*'". I have argued that there is such a thing as behaving like one who says "Let's eat," "Please, let me go to bed", and so on. Thus I am now entitled to speak of desirings that are characterized by "Let's eat", "Please, let me go to bed", and so on, or in more colloquial language, of cases of people desiring to eat, to go to bed, and so on.

There is, of course, no need in most contexts to spell out the normalcies that are exhibited in our daily life. I shall in fact now generally speak in the language of desiring, which is convenient, obvious, and often truistic. It was only necessary to proceed so slowly in the context of the circularity problem. In particular, it was necessary to show that we could explain the reason for associating a certain kind of behavior with a certain sentence in terms of normalcies and without reference to prior assignments of thinkings.

Our task now is to extend the idea developed in the last three paragraphs to a wider class of cases. We may consider an imperative that is associated with a less general interest than the ones just reviewed. For example, people who say "Please pass the potatoes" at table usually eat some of the potatoes that shortly arrive. While the potatoes are being passed they do not normally rise from their places, fold their napkins or pat their stomachs and say "I'm stuffed." So there is something that people would reasonably expect if they were told that you would behave like a person who says "Please pass the potatoes" or, what comes to the same by (TTA), if they were told that you want the potatoes passed.

I turn now to some declarative utterances. People who say "Candidate X is the best one" around election time usually vote for candidate X if they vote at all. Politicians who say things like "Bill #191 provides more benefits at less cost than any alternative proposal that is likely to pass" and say it close to the time at which the vote on the bill is to be taken usually vote for Bill #191. So there is a reason that can be described by reference to normalcies and without reference to other thinkings for associating yea-voting with people who say the things just quoted. There is thus a non-circular reason for identifying something as behaving like a person who says such things. By (TTA) we are non-circularly justified in speaking of believings characterized by the above sentences or, more colloquially, of cases of believing that candidate X is the best one or that Bill #191 has certain features.

These examples suggest a complication that we must discuss. Notoriously, politicians break their promises or change their minds. So a politician who speaks in favor of Bill #191 now may very well vote against it in a few months. This might get one to thinking that, after all, there is no behavior that is associated with speaking in behalf of Bill #191. There are, however, two things that can be said about this. First, the very fact that we speak of broken promises or changes of mind shows that we do in fact associate a certain kind of behavior with sentences of the kind I used as an example. This is possible because, as is built into (NEU), we take account of circumstances in which things are said and not only the utterances themselves. Second, there are *some* concomitants of speaking as I have imagined that are normal no matter what the circumstances. Thus, people who speak of the benefits of a bill hardly ever villify others who speak on its behalf; they do not oppose other measures that serve ends similar to the bill they favor without being a rival to it; they do not simultaneously oppose ends that the bill they support would serve. These facts are, of course, special cases of the truism that people generally act coherently, that is, they do not normally act in such a way that one thing they do prevents the normal effect of something else they do from serving their desires.

I have been arguing that, for many p, there is such a thing as behaving like a person who says "p". It will be useful for further development to give this result a more formal expression. We can state the point as a Relation between Behavior and Utterance:

(RBU)   For many p, there is at least one circumstance C such that
   (i) C can be specified without reference to utterers' thinkings, and
   (ii) There is some behavior B such that normally, when people say "p" in C, they exhibit B.

There are some believings for which a wider condition (ii) would hold. An example would be "$2 + 2 = 4$." Teachers routinely say this and we could illustrate (RBU) by choosing for C a case where an adding of 2 and 2 is about to take place. Then B would be the writing or speaking of "4". But it is also true that teachers who say "$2 + 2 = 4$" can be counted on to add correctly if a case of adding 2 and 2 comes up in the future. This suggests an alternative to (ii), as follows:

> (ii′)   There is some behavior B such that normally, if people say "p," then they exhibit B upon the subsequent occurrence of C.

Let us give the name "(RBU′)" to a statement just like (RBU) except that it has (ii′) instead of (ii). It is obvious that (RBU′) holds for many p, although, as the example of the politicians' behavior shows, it holds for fewer p than does (RBU). Since (RBU) and (RBU′) are both true, let us conjoin them. We may call the result "(RBU$_1$)".

(RBU$_1$) has been introduced as part of our argument that there is such a thing as behaving like a person who says "p". In order to go on and complete our argument and our explanation of what behaving like a person who says "p" comes to, we need to look at (RBU$_1$) from another point of view. We need to notice that (RBU$_1$) can be used to describe the kind of evidence that is relevant to establishing that people have a thinking characterizable by p. That is, we can read (RBU$_1$) as telling us that when people exhibit behavior B in circumstance C, they are acting like people who say "p". So, if we observe people exhibiting B and C, we have reason to characterize them as behaving like those who say "p". That is, by (TTA), we have reason to attribute to them a thinking characterized by "p". For many attributions of thinkings, evidence of the kind just described will be sufficient to provide us with as much certainty as we can ever have about contingent facts. Since we will need to refer to the ps that characterize thinkings for which such evidence is sufficient, I shall introduce a short phrase to denote them. I shall call them "p that can be established by (RBU$_1$)".

While some p can be established by (RBU$_1$) alone, there are some p for which something more is involved than what is captured in (RBU$_1$). We can bring this out by noting that for many p, there is more to behaving like a person who says "p" than doing what is normal for everyone in some circumstance. Sometimes one also has to do what normal people would do if they not only said "p" *but also had certain other thinkings characterized by, say, q or r.* For example, Jones is not behaving like someone who says "Smith has arrived" unless she takes steps to avoid encountering him—for I am supposing that she finds Smith obnoxious. People who find Smith obnoxious would normally take steps to avoid him when they believe he has arrived; but, of course, this does not hold of all normal people without further specification. This point may seem to reintroduce the circularity problem; but I shall now explain how we can accommodate it without falling afoul of this problem. Intuitively, the strategy of the formulations I shall give is to use thinkings that can be established by (RBU_1) to help establish further thinkings; then to use these to establish still further ones; and so on. The conception I am working toward is that we can begin with basic needs in order to establish some desires; that we can use these to establish some beliefs about the immediate situation; that we can use these in turn to establish further desires and beliefs; and that we can gradually spiral outward toward the establishing of a person's whole belief/desire hierarchy. We can give this strategy formal expression by modifying (i) in (RBU_1). We then obtain:

(RBU_2) For many p, there is at least one C such that

(i') C can be specified in a way that refers to no thinkings T^x of utterers of p except those such that

    (a) T^x is characterized by p^x and

    (b) p^x is a p that can be established by (RBU_1); and

(ii'')   Either there is some behavior B such that normally when people say "p" in C they exhibit B or there is some behavior B such that normally when people say "p" then if C occurs, they exhibit B.[11]

11. That is, one (or both) of the conditions (ii) or (ii') holds.

Once again, while (RBU$_2$) has been introduced to articulate the concept of behaving like a person who says "p", we can regard it as a description of how we can establish that people are behaving in this way and thus, by (TTA), as a description of how we can establish that people have certain thinkings. I shall refer to the p that characterize such thinkings as "p that can be established by (RBU$_2$)".

We can now formulate (RBU$_3$), which is just like (RBU$_2$) except that clause (*b*) of condition (i′) reads

> (*b*) p^x is a p that can be established by (RBU$_1$) or (RBU$_2$).

Generalizing this idea, we can formulate a series of statements in which each (RBU$_n$) has a clause (*b*) of condition (i′) that reads

> (*b*) p^x is a p that can be established by (RBU$_1$) or . . . or (RBU$_{n-1}$).

This enables us to formulate a Solution to the Circularity Problem.

> (SCP)   Every thinking for whose attribution we have good reason is characterized by a p such that, for some n, p can be established by (RBU$_n$).

I have argued for the truth of (RBU$_1$). A direct argument for (SCP), however, would require us to take an arbitrary attribution that we regard as well founded and work out all the (RBU$_n$) that would come up in the course of establishing it. One case of this might require a whole book. So (SCP) must remain an hypothesis. It has the following properties. It does not appeal to anything non-physical. It solves the circularity problem. It begins with something that can be convincingly argued for (that is, (RBU$_1$)). It enables us to make theoretical sense of the obvious fact that we use assumptions about some of people's thinkings in order to establish further attributions of thinkings to them. Finally, when we see some of the difficulties of alternative views, I believe (SCP) will emerge as by far

the most reasonable view to take about our attributions of thinkings.

Some Consequences

Before considering alternatives, I want to return to the notion of
pretending that someone has said "p" and exhibit its fruitfulness.
This will enable me to complete my account of intentionality and to
respond to some natural questions. There are three topics that I will
take up.

(i) In an early section of this chapter, I described two ways of
introducing the concept of intentionality. The second of these depends on the fact that certain inferences fail, even though they involve the mere substitution of names or phrases that denote the
same things as the words they replace. On my account we can understand the peculiarity of these inferences as derivative upon intentionality in the sense of its first, more fundamental introduction. In
general, knowledge that N_1 is identical with N_2 (or that the G is
identical with the H) is independent of knowledge that N_1 is F (or
that the G is F) or that N_2 is F (or that the H is F). Thus people who
say "N_1 is F" (or "The G is F") may or may not behave like people
who say "N_2 is F" (or "The H is F"). Therefore, pretending that
people have said one of these things will in general be different from
pretending that they have said the others. Or, by (TTA), attributing
to people a thinking characterized by one of the above sentences is
different from attributing to them a thinking characterized by one of
the others.

These remarks may draw the objection that they are too strong,
because they fail to recognize that some attributions of thinkings do
not exhibit the inferential peculiarity noted above.[12] I have in mind
here *de re* beliefs and desires. However, we can easily add an account of these. For simplicity I shall state this account only for *de re*

12. This objection was brought to my attention by Thomas C. Ryckman.

beliefs; the account for *de re* desires will be an obvious parallel. To begin with, it will be helpful to have a standard form for attributions of both *de re* and *de dicto* beliefs. For the first, I shall use the schema

(DRB)   *P* asserts that *S* believes, with respect to *a*, that it is *F* (where *a* is a referring expression).

For the second, I shall use the schema

(DDB)   *P* asserts that *S* believes that *a* is *F* (where, again, *a* is a referring expression).

Let us suppose that we can lay aside (or settle) any questions about the sincerity of *P*. Then, if we know an instance of (DDB) we have some reason to pretend that *S* has said "*a* is *F*." We can think of *P* as inviting us to adopt this pretence. However, if we know an instance of (DRB) we know less about what we should pretend about *S*. We can take *P* to be inviting us to pretend that *S* has said something of the form "*x* is *F*", but we don't know what we should put in the place of "*x*". On the other hand, in knowing an instance of (DRB) we get to know more about *P*. We are entitled to pretend that *P* has said something of the form "*a* is . . . " without knowing how we should fill in the dots. In knowing an instance of (DDB), of course, we do not have any guide to what we should pretend with respect to *P*. We can sum up these remarks by saying that *de re* belief-attributions "put us in the picture" with respect to both attributor and attributee—at the cost of telling us less about the attributee. *De dicto* attributions tell us more about the attributee, but nothing about the attributor.[13]

(ii) I have been arguing that the meaning of utterances depends on their normal effects and that, in consequence, normal people speak as they do in part because they anticipate the effects of their utter-

13. Except, of course, whatever follows from *P*'s being an attributor of anything at all to *S*.

ances. In turn, when we hear people speak, or hear reports of what they say, we have responses and expectations that are appropriate to people who are expecting such effects and who are unlikely to do things that might interfere with those effects.

Conditions are, however, not always normal. It is worth commenting on a few cases in which something unusual is afoot. The comments to come will provide a background for the statement of, and also the resolution of, a problem that some will want to raise against a physicalistic account of intentionality.

We can be misled by half truth. A special case of this can be described as follows. Suppose a thinking characterizable by p would be normal for people in S's position to have, but that S in fact thinks not-p. On being told, quite correctly, that S also thinks in a way characterizable by q, we may come to expect a certain behavior from S that will not actually be forthcoming. Our error can be corrected (or prevented) by learning more about S, that is, by learning about S's unusual thinking.

The case just described is one in which the responses mobilized by an attribution of a thinking are inappropriate. In another kind of case, they may be merely not forthcoming. Most people would, for example, have very little response upon hearing that Jones believes that there are universals. There is hardly anything that would strike them as surprising in view of what they've heard (or hardly anything whose occurrence or non-occurrence *becomes* surprising because they have heard this attribution). Similar remarks would hold for any thinking whose characterizing sentence involves a piece of jargon. As before, increased response, increased understanding, and increased usefulness of having heard attributions all come with increased knowledge. In the cases at hand, making use of an attribution requires learning the jargon in which the sentence characterizing it is expressed. One must, for example, develop some habits of response to utterances involving the term "universal". If one is to understand correctly, these habits of response must parallel those possessed by members of the linguistic subcommunity in which such utterances are common. It is only when one has such habits that they can be mobilized in pretending that people have said something about universals.

The same point can be extended to the case of utterances made by speakers of a language we do not understand. Such utterances will have no effect on us, except in so far as they are noises or expenditures of energy on the part of the speaker. In order to make any further use of them, we can do one of two things. First, we may learn the other language; that is, we may come to have the same normal responses to utterances in it that are had by its native speakers. If we do this, we will also be able to understand attributions of thinkings to people, where the sentences characterizing the thinkings are sentences of the new language. The alternative procedure is to rely on a translation of utterances of the new language into our familiar one. In this case we pretend that the speaker of the new language has said something in our language. We allow our normal expectations and responses to be mobilized in reference to the speaker. If our expectations are correct and our responses are successful, we will count the translation as a good one.[14]

This scheme of things is simple enough as long as the new language and our familiar one are in perfect correspondence. That is, matters are simple so long as there are normal responses by native speakers of the new language that match our normal responses to our translations of their utterances. But what if the correspondence breaks down? What if members of another community normally believe something that would be deviant in our community? This might have the consequences that no utterance in our language would have the same normal consequences as any utterance in the new language, and vice versa. In this case, pretending that a speaker had said "p", where p is a sentence of our language, would always lead us to mistaken expectations.

14. This is a place at which my debt to Wilfrid Sellars should be particularly obvious.

Fortunately, we are versatile beings who can pretend a number of things at the same time. (This is a consequence of the fact that we can adjust our actual behavior to any number of features of a situation—which is just a way of saying we are intelligent.) We can pretend that people say "*p*" while, at the same time, pretending that they say "*q*". *We can pretend both of these while also pretending* that they respond to our utterances as we do except in some certain respect—much as we can pretend to be a person in a hurry, but also pretend to be a person who is in a hurry but has a damaged knee. The more we know about the people whom we are trying to understand through translation, the closer our pretendings can get to being appropriate in every respect to the behavior they will exhibit.

The full development in this direction makes us able to respond to an utterance either as our real selves or as people who are normal members of another community. With this ability goes the ability to anticipate[15] others' responses to one's utterances. These abilities make possible criticism of the kind I will call "insightful". Insightful criticism is criticism of the kind that could be immediately understood, and appreciated as criticism, by the people being criticized. It is to be contrasted with superficial criticism, which merely rejects the unfamiliar because it is not like what is familiar.[16] Insightful criticism is possible because we can learn to respond like a member of another community; we can come to appreciate what would be considered a *problem* by normal members of a new community, what would be considered to be a response to it, and what would be a satisfying response by their lights.

We are now in a position where we can state and discuss an objection to our whole account. This objection asserts that in order to understand people in another community we must understand what

15. Recall that anticipating is not rehearsal or conscious articulation of predictions, but only becoming disposed to be surprised by possible future occurrences and the ability to adjust one's behavior to be successful in normal cases. See above, p. 98.

16. Or, less commonly, accepts something because it accords with something already found desirable.

their cultural form demands of them. For example, to understand something said by a feudal lord, it would be necessary to understand feudalism. To understand something said by a Hindu, it would be necessary to understand that religion and to know what its internal structure imposes upon those who subscribe to it. The objection further asserts that such cultural forms transcend the behavior of individuals and cannot be reduced in any other way to the purely physical. If this is so, the full understanding of intentionality requires something that, while it is perhaps not mental, is certainly not physical.[17]

In response to this objection, I agree that there is a sense in which cultural forms are independent of the behavior of the individuals composing a community. I deny, however, that this kind of independence requires an ontological commitment to anything non-physical. The key point in making out this position is the claim that the independence of cultural forms is nothing other than the fact that (insightful) criticism in a community is never finished. The members of a community can never be in a position to know that no further objection, question, or problem can arise for their beliefs and habits of action. When we pretend to be members of a community, we are no better off in principle than its actual members. We can never reasonably suppose that we have thought of all the challenges to a way of living that could be raised from within the community itself. However, we *can* raise challenges that *were not* actually raised by members of a community. If we have understood the community well, we can successfully pretend to give responses of its members to problems we have pretended to have been raised. If *we* can agree on what a well-considered response by typical members of a community would have been, we can legitimately treat the response as "built into" the cultural form of that community, even if it was never called forth in the actual history of its members. In drawing such a conclu-

17. This objection was called to my attention by A. Anthony Smith.

sion we are, in effect, using the same abilities as were possessed by members of the community under consideration—abilities that we have been able to acquire by thorough study of their actual behavior. It is in the nature of abilities to have potential for being exercised on occasions other than those on which they are actually used. It is this fact, not any non-physical thing, that explains the independence of cultural forms.

(iii) Intentionality is often attributed to animals and occasionally to simple devices such as thermostats. Such attributions strike some people as compelling, but others as vastly oversympathetic to animals or as downright ridiculous. Some ideas already introduced will enable us to make sense of these conflicting intuitions.

The problem presented by animals is that it seems natural to attribute thinkings to them; the only way we have of characterizing those thinkings is by sentences of our language; but we do not at all wish to imply that animals understand our language. The solution to this problem lies in the fact that we can adjust our pretendings to several features of our situation at the same time. Thus, we can pretend that our dog has said "I want to go out" or "There are Dog Crunchies in that cupboard." That is, we can suppose that it will behave like a person who says those things *while taking account of the fact that we are pretending this of a dog.* Our expectations will be adjusted accordingly and our responses will be appropriate to the fact that Fido is a dog as well as to the fact that it wants to go out. People who want to go out get up, put their coats on, and open the door. We do not ordinarily offer them assistance. If they are children or paralyzed we do offer assistance. We factor these features into our behavior. I am proposing that this is also the way in which we can make sense of attributions of thinkings to animals.

We can run the same idea with respect to a thermostat. We can pretend that it has just said "It's cold in here" or we can pretend that it will behave like a person who has just said "It's cold in here"— bearing in mind that it is a thermostat about which we are pretending. We *can* do this: that is what, on my view, enables us to make sense of the fact that we *can* talk of thermostats in intentional terms. The intuition that such talk is silly corresponds to the fact that there isn't much to do to pretend of a thermostat that it has said "It's cold in here"; it is just going to make a contact that closes a circuit and that is that. If we had said simply that it is about to make such a contact, we would have conveyed everything we conveyed by saying "It thinks it's cold in here." By contrast, pretending that animals have thinkings is much richer. For example, what Fido will do if it wants to go out will be different depending on what kind of barrier it has to surmount, whether its master is present, and how long it has been since its last outing.

Inner Speech

Inner speech is that which is often referred to by the phrases "internal monologue" and "silent soliloquy". It is conducted in some definite language. It takes approximately as long to say something in inner speech as it does to say it in audible speech. One can inwardly speak casually or pompously, with or without emphasis, in one's customary accent or in imitation of someone else's. It is inner speech to which bilingual people refer when they make remarks like "You know, after all these years I still count to myself in my native German."

Inner speech is easily distinguishable from strings of auditory sensations. In normal cases, the latter would be caused by audible sounds. In an abnormal case, we might call auditory sensations "hearing voices" rather than "inner speech". However, the words of inner speech are like sensations in that they occur at definite times and literally have some of the same properties as those possessed by the words of heard voices, for example, exemplifying a certain accent, being monotone or else rising and falling, and being composed of vowels and consonants in a certain order.

The words of inner speech are also like sensations in that the arguments for dualism given in Chapter I apply *mutatis mutandis* to them. I will spell this out very briefly. Application of the reducibility principle (page 27) tells us that if the words of inner speech were composed of firing neurons, their properties would have to be explainable by reference to the properties and relations of those neurons. But firing ratios or patterns or intensities do not explain why a bit of inner speech should have the property of being an inner speech "A" sound or an inner speech "T" sound. We might be able to correlate occurrences of certain kinds of neuron firings with certain bits of inner speech, but the former would not enable us to see why the latter should have the properties they have. One might suggest a topic-neutral approach that would identify neuron firings with inner speech on the ground that "both" are causes of audible speech or other behavior. It will soon be evident, however, why this suggestion will not work. Finally, the properties of the words of inner speech do not have distance-dependent effects. Thus we cannot suppose that we will find inner speech introduced into the science of the future in such a way as to give it a straightforwardly spatial location.

The similarities and differences between inner speech and auditory sensations to which I have called attention in the last two paragraphs justify the application of the term "auditory imagery" to inner speech. There are, of course, other kinds of auditory imagery, that is, items for which the above remarks would hold but that do not come in words. A tune "running around in one's head" is an example. This is also an example of auditory imagery that does not have intentionality. The auditory imagery that comes in words, however, does have intentionality; that is why we have to discuss it here. The central point to be made about this intentionality is that it is nothing but the intentionality of the words that occur in inner speech. If argument for this is needed we can observe that auditory imagery without a surrounding linguistic context would lack intentionality. "Urk malng pfizit" is not about anything, whether I say it out loud or whether I have it in auditory imagery. But for all I know, the same imagery had by a Martian would be a rehearsal of a very improper invitation. The circumstances required for this to be the case are just that these sounds would be an improper invitation if the Martian said them out loud back home.

If this is right it is extremely doubtful that inner speech is a cause of audible speech or of actions. For I am claiming that inner speech has its intentionality derivatively. It could thus never have had any point—could not have been inwardly *saying* anything—unless there had already been audible speech and normal responses to audible utterances. At some time, therefore, these latter must have had causes other than inner speech. It is extremely implausible to suppose that somehow these causes have been replaced in their function by inner speech. There is, moreover, obvious evidence against such an hypothesis. When we converse, we do not have inner speech rehearsals of what we say. Nor do we need inner speech rehearsals of our actions, any more than we need to say out loud what we are going to do before we do it. Further, when we do have inner speech rehearsals of what we are about to say our actual utterances are usually improvements upon, rather than exact repetitions of, our inner speech. Finally, all these facts are very plausibly accounted for by the supposition that inner speech is an effect of causes that are largely the same as those that produce overt speech. For these reasons, we should resist identifications, like that made by Jerry Fodor, of mental causes and "what is running through one's head".[18]

At the beginning of my account of intentionality I claimed that while I would have to mention something non-physical, the contri-

18. See Jerry Fodor, "Methodological Solipsism Considered as a Research Strategy in Cognitive Psychology", reprinted in his *Representations* (Cambridge, Mass.: MIT Press, 1981), pp. 225–253. For the illicit identification see esp. pp. 235–236, 237, and 246.

bution that this makes would be clearly parasitic on a grounding of intentionality that did not appeal to anything non-physical. In arguing that the intentionality of inner speech is derivative upon the intentionality of audible speech I have supported and explained this claim.

CHAPTER IV

Acts and Thoughts

I have tried to make the foregoing account of intentionality as simple as possible. It has to be recognized, however, that it has a certain amount of complexity. Some alternative views of intentionality have the advantage of being much simpler. This can become a powerful reason for being attracted to them. It is thus necessary to present the most important of these views and to show that the price they pay for simplicity is too high.

The alternatives that we must consider share something besides (relative) simplicity. They are ways of expanding on the idea that words are meaningful because they *express* our *thoughts*. This is also a powerful attraction of these views, and we must show why it does not really give us a reason for preferring them. The process of getting out from under the idea that words are meaningful because they express thoughts will enable us to see more clearly what the view of the preceding chapter amounts to and will allow us to have a firmer grasp of how our conception of ourselves as thinkers can be related to our conception of ourselves as dependent on neural activity.

Intrinsic Intentionality and Acts

In order to understand the first of our alternative views we must make a distinction between *intrinsic* and *extrinsic* intentionality. I shall say that an item that has intentionality has it extrinsically just in case its having intentionality (or, its having its particular intentionality, for example, meaning or standing for whatever exactly it does mean or stand for) depends on its standing in relation to some other things. I shall say that an item has its intentionality intrinsically if its having intentionality (or its particular intentionality) does not depend on its standing in relation to other things.

The view I have presented in Chapter III recognizes nothing that has its intentionality intrinsically. The alternative I now want to discuss diverges from that view precisely by holding that some items do have their intentionality intrinsically. It holds, further, that the items that have intrinsic intentionality are thoughts, in exactly my regimented sense of an "inner episode". Interestingly enough, we may take this as our entire specification of the view to be considered. Even though there are a number of further questions that arise, it turns out that it doesn't matter how we answer them: the criticisms I will make will apply whatever answer we give. We should, however, mention one or two of the possible sub-alternatives. Thus, we can ask whether or not thoughts are "inner" in the literal sense of inside the head. An affirmative answer here has not often been advanced, because this would commit one to something straightforwardly physical with intrinsic intentionality.[1] The usual answer has been

---

1. John Searle appears to embrace intrinsically intentional physical things in his *Intentionality* (Cambridge: Cambridge University Press, 1983). Such a view is suggested by putting the following quotations together. "In my view it is not possible to give a logical analysis of the Intentionality of the mental in terms of simpler notions, since Intentionality is, so to speak, a ground floor property of the mind, not a logically complex feature built up by combining simpler elements" (26). "[I]f the question is "What is the mode of existence of beliefs and other Intentional states?" then from everything we currently know about how the world works the answer is: Intentional states are both caused by and realized in the structure of the brain" (15). However, Searle also says, "An Intentional state only determines its conditions of satisfaction—and thus only is the state that it is—given its position in a *Network* of other Intentional states and against a *Background* of practices and preintentional assumptions that are neither themselves Intentional states nor are they parts of the

the negative one, that is, the view that thoughts are non-physical, mental episodes having intrinsic intentionality, which are "inner" only in the metaphorical sense of somehow "standing behind" our behavior. The traditional name for items conceived in this way is "(mental) act" and I shall use this term in the remainder of this section.[2] One may now ask whether or not the intrinsic intentionality of an act can be analyzed into two facts, namely, (a) the fact that an act is an individual with a certain property and (b) the fact that the *property* has intrinsic intentionality. I shall adopt the simpler mode of speaking; that is, I shall say that acts are what have intentionality. Everything I will say, however, can be trivially reformulated to apply to the view that holds that, strictly speaking, it is properties of acts that have intentionality.[3]

I shall not attempt to argue that there are no acts. I shall, however, argue that we do not need them. The reason people believe they are needed is that without them, it seems, words would not be expressing our thoughts. But if words did not express our thoughts, they would be meaningless noises. They could not have intentionality. We can make the same point starting from the other end. There is nothing about noises or series of letters by themselves that bestows a

conditions of satisfaction of Intentional states" (19). This and the ensuing discussion seem to imply that the intentionality of brain structures logically depends on their standing in certain relations to certain kinds of other things, that is, that their intentionality is *not* intrinsic in the sense in which I am using the term. I have been unable to satisfy myself that there is any clear resolution of these opposing tendencies in Searle's work; hence I find the classification of his view problematic.

2. "Mental act" in philosophy of mind has no special connection with will, although deciding is a species of act. (Other species include believing, desiring, fearing, wondering, and many more.) "Mental act" does *not* derive from "mental action" or "mental activity". Instead it means "mental actuality", that is, "actually existing mental state or event".

3. For an exposition of an act view, see Gustav Bergmann, "Acts", in his *Logic and Reality* (Madison: University of Wisconsin Press, 1964). See also Roderick Chisholm's correspondence with Wilfrid Sellars in *Minnesota Studies in the Philosophy of Science*, vol. 2 (1958), pp. 521–539.

meaning on them; if there were, translation would be impossible (how could those other sounds mean the same thing as ours?) and perhaps unnecessary (because there would be only one thing the foreigner's sounds *could* mean). These consequences are, of course, absurd. But then, words must be *given* a meaning. It can seem obvious that we give them a meaning by *using* them to express our thoughts. This, however, requires that there be thoughts that already have their intentionality.

Plausible as this may be, it is incoherent. We cannot make sense of the idea that an intrinsically intentional act contributes anything to the intentionality of language. To bring this out we must ask the question whether sincere statements that involve no verbal slip could mis-express what their utterers' mental acts are about. Suppose, first, that this is logically impossible. This supposition destroys the *intrinsic* intentionality of acts, because according to it they *could not* mean what they mean unless they were related to certain behaviors on the part of the people who have them. (The relation would be this. *If* people say "The cat is on the mat" when they are intending to say what's on their minds, then (on this first supposition) they *must* be having an act that is about the cat being on the mat. The converse is that if they are having that act, then it is logically necessary that *if* they intend to say what's on their minds, and they actually speak and do not suffer a slip of the tongue, *then* they say "The cat is on the mat" or at least something synonymous with this.) This, however, makes the intentionality of acts dependent on their relation to behavior; and this is incompatible with their having their intentionality intrinsically. So let us move to the alternative supposition, that it is logically possible for a sincere utterance without a verbal slip to mis-express what an act is about. This supposition cuts against the idea that my utterances derive their intentionality from my acts. For a *mis*-expression has to be directed upon something *other* than what the accompanying act is directed upon. But then, its being directed upon whatever it *is* directed upon cannot be supposed to derive from the act that accompanies it. Therefore, the meaning of the utterance gets its direction from something other than the accompanying act.

One response that might be made to this argument is to say that utterances that do not express accompanying acts cannot really express anything different, that they must really be nonsense and at best appear to express something different. This is unintelligible, however, since there is no sense to the claim that somebody's utterance of "The cat is on the mat" (for example) is really nonsense and only appears to mean something. A stronger response would be to hold that it is logically necessary that our words *usually* express our acts. However, if it is not necessary for each sincere, non-verbally-slipped utterance to correspond to its utterer's act, we can ask for an explanation of this general necessity. There is no plausible idea that is relevant here, except for the idea that language could not function unless people normally said what they thought. However, this idea cannot support an act view, because it can be accounted for by alternatives. It is, in fact, incorporated in the view of Chapter III. (If this is not already obvious, it will become so very shortly.) Thus we are entitled to the conclusion I anticipated above, that is, that a view that embraces intrinsically intentional acts cannot be something that we need in order to account for the meaningfulness of our words.

If we are to overcome completely the attraction of the view we have been discussing, we must give an alternative account of the consideration that makes it plausible. The grain of truth behind the temptation to say that our words must express our acts is that it is necessary for meaningful words generally to express our *thinkings*. We can make this out as follows. Sounds would be meaningless unless they were located in surroundings in which their utterance had normal effects on hearers. They could not be understood if people were not able to react to the circumstance that these effects are the normal ones. In particular, they could not be understood if people who uttered them did not normally anticipate the likely results of their utterances and did not adjust their utterances to those anticipated results. However, if people do anticipate and adjust in this way, with respect to some utterance p, then there will be something that counts as behaving like a person who says "p". Thus (cf. (TTA)) there will be the grounds required for attributing a thinking characterizable by p. Conversely, where there are thinkings characterizable by p, there must be such a thing as behaving like a person who says "p" and hence utterances of p must have normal effects on hearers. The connection between thinkings and words can be summed up in this way: Necessarily, words generally express our thinkings because the conditions required for there being thinkings are the same as those required for there being meaningful words. A sentence etched into rocks by the wind would fail to be an utterance, not because there would be no act for it to express, but because the conditions for its being an expression of some person's thinking would be lacking.

There is one more way in which intrinsically intentional acts may be introduced. It may be held that, whether or not we need them in order to explain anything, we have non-inferential and incorrigible knowledge of our acts or, in short, that we are acquainted with them. I cannot prove that the concept of an act with which we are acquainted is self-contradictory and I cannot add anything to what I have already said to cast doubt on the coherence of the very idea of a mental act "behind" our words. But I can try to explain why some people might falsely believe they are acquainted with acts. There are three possible confusions about which I shall comment. (i) We can easily produce statements of the form "I believe that p" or "I desire that q be the case." Moreover, when we say these things we can know that they are true. These statements have more words than do p or q by themselves. So it may seem that they must refer to something besides what is referred to by p or q. Acts with which we are acquainted would answer to the description of something further, which the longer statements could be about and which would account for the fact that we can know those longer statements to be true. What we must notice, however, is that the actual force of "I believe that p" and "I desire that q be the case" is only an intensification of "p" and "Let q be the case", respectively. Utterances of the former do not tell hearers any more about my thinkings than do utterances of the latter. We do not need to know or be acquainted with anything further in order to know the former than we do to know the latter. The fact that we can know that "I believe that p" is true without investigating the world or calculating my future behavior requires no more than what is already required by the fact that I can utter "p" and then go on to behave like someone who says "p". Normally, if language is to have meaning, those who say "p" must behave like people who say "p"; that is, there must be something that counts as behaving like one who says "p". So, normally, people who say "p" in an intensified manner will behave like people who say "p"; that is, their self-ascriptions of thinkings will normally match their future behavior.

(ii) There is an experience that is naturally described as "fishing for words" to express what one wants to say. When one finds them it can seem as if one has finally found the words that match what has been "before one's mind" all along. It is tempting to represent a case of this kind as one in which one is acquainted with one's act and knows what one's act is about during the time that one is searching for the right words. However, this way of representing the situation says more than we are entitled to say. The fact that something seems correct does not show that it matches something that was already there. It can perfectly well be the case that some attempts to articulate one's thinkings have results that lead us to reject them as incorrect and that the "correct" expression is merely the one that no longer strikes us as having unwanted consequences.

(iii) We are acquainted with our inner speech. This gives us a way in which we can tell ourselves what we think. Through this, we can come to have a sense that what we think is immediately present to us. This, I suggest, may be one fact that leads to the plausibility of intrinsically intentional acts. We have, however, already seen that inner speech has its intentionality derivatively; that is, it is about whatever the words composing it are about. Thus, it does not have its intentionality intrinsically. Acquaintance with our inner speech, therefore, cannot be acquaintance with intrinsically intentional mental acts.

Extrinsically Intentional Thoughts

The views I will now discuss differ from the account of Chapter III by holding that the analysis of intentionality requires internal episodes having intentionality. They differ from the view of the preceding section by holding that the required internal episodes do not have their intentionality intrinsically. These internal episodes are thus not acts and I shall refer to them by the term I have already regimented for the purpose, that is, "thoughts". There is a further, subsidiary difference. Since the thoughts we are now considering have their intentionality extrinsically, there is no longer any motive for supposing they are non-physical. In conformity to actually held views, I shall assume in what follows that thoughts are to be identified with brain states.

If thoughts are said to have their intentionality extrinsically, we can ask what relations are involved and what things thoughts must be related to in order to be intentional. The interesting answers to this question are two. The Etiological View is

(EV) Thoughts derive their intentionality from certain features of their causes.

The alternative, Consequentialist View is

(CV) Thoughts derive their intentionality from certain features of their effects.

I shall discuss these alternatives in the following two sections.

Etiology

The etiological view has been articulated and persuasively argued for by Fred Dretske. His is clearly the strongest version of the view and I shall henceforth identify (EV) with Dretske's way of developing it. Since I will be quoting some of Dretske's arguments in a critical context it seems only fair to expound the view in his own words.

> A system *has* concepts insofar as its internal states constitute an alignment, some degree of coordination, between input and output. But the fact that there exists this kind of coordination between input and output does not determine *what concepts* a system has. What concepts a system has depends on what kind of information it is *to which* the coordination has been made (214).[4] . . . A concept is a two faced structure: one face looks backward to informational origins; the other face looks ahead to effects and consequences. No structure qualifies as a concept unless it has both the backward-looking, informational aspect and the forward-looking, functional aspect, but what gives the structure its conceptual identity, what makes it *this* concept rather than *that* concept, is its etiological specificity (214–215). . . . What I have argued is that our internal states acquire their meaning in terms of the information to which their original formation into functional units was a response. It is the information embodied in these original, formative stimuli that supplies the content to those internal structures (231).

Before turning to Dretske's arguments for this view two preliminary remarks are in order. (i) In the portion of Dretske's work that we are about to consider it is taken for granted that there are thoughts and

---

4. Parenthetical numbers in this subsection refer to pages of Fred Dretske, *Knowledge and the Flow of Information* (Cambridge, Mass.: MIT Press, 1981).

the question at issue is how they acquire their particular intentionality. My account of intentionality does not require the introduction of thoughts, so I regard their use as contentious. It would, however, be tedious to repeat this, so I will pretend to go along with thoughts while considering the etiological view. My strategy in the long run is to show that thoughts cannot help us account for intentionality by showing that first, (EV) is false and second, (CV) prevents thoughts from making any contribution to the analysis of intentionality. (ii) (CV) is a claim about thoughts, but many things that can be said about it could be applied to my view that the intentionality of utterances depends on their normal consequences. Dretske sometimes states his case against (CV) in broad terms: he thinks that not only can thoughts not acquire their intentionality from their effects, but that nothing can. It should be clear from each context what items are being denied to acquire their intentionality from their effects.

My discussion of (EV) will fall into three stages. First, I shall present an argument against it. Second, I shall consider Dretske's positive arguments in favor of his view. Lastly, I shall turn to arguments that seek to support Dretske's position by refuting the consequentialist alternative.

Suppose my body were so arranged that I had a small, brief spasm in a muscle in my left forearm whenever a red thing came into my visual field. This is not impossible. There are, after all, retinal states produced by red things. There is *something* that is common to the effects of such states, even if it is only our ability to report what has come into our visual field by using the same word, "red". It is logically possible that, in some human perceiver, whatever allows us to apply the same word to red things got accidentally connected to a neuron leading to a left forearm muscle. Of course, learning to apply "red" in the normal course of things involves learning some language. But the kind of connection we are imagining *could* have been brought about by some fantastically improbable series of accidents.[5] So let us suppose that the tic in my forearm has arisen in such a way. Further, let us imagine that I have not been trained to make use of this tic as a sign of red things. Let us suppose, finally, that I do not understand the word "red" or any synonym and that I cannot successfully respond to requests to bring red things, shoot red things, and so on.

We must add certain specifications to this case in order to match some technical requirements laid down by Dretske. We can do this in a way that is compatible with what we have imagined so far. Thus, consider the brain event S, which causes the firing of the neuron that in turn causes my muscle to have a spasm. S carries the information that the object before me is red.[6] Further, it may be assumed to carry this information in completely digitalized form.[7]

5. To deny this is to commit oneself to the view that what Dretske's etiological account requires for intentionality logically could not be met unless the effects required by the consequentialist account are generated. This *prima facie* unattractive position muddies the waters and leaves us with only the arguments to be discussed below as relevant considerations.

6. It does so *ex hypothesi*. "Information" is a technical term, which Dretske explains at length. Not every detail is relevant here and I will not digress by attempting to summarize Dretske's discussion. The main point is that conditions can be such that I would not be having S unless something red had just entered my visual field. Skeptical problems that might be raised against this possibility are the same as those that might be raised against the possibility of ever knowing that a red thing has come before me. Dretske says a number of things in reply to such skepticism; I shall assume for the sake of the argument that he is successful.

7. "[W]e redefine a structure's semantic content as that piece of information it carries in (what I shall call) *completely digitalized form* i.e.,

> Structure S has the fact that t is F as its semantic
> content =
> (a) S carries the information that t is F and
> (b) S carries no other piece of information, r is G,
> which is such that the information that t is F is
> nested (nomically or analytically) in r's being G"
> $(184-185)$.

That is, S may be produced in somewhat different ways depending on the object's shape or shade of red or intensity. If this is the case, S will carry no information about those other matters, nor about other neural states that may have produced it in a particular case. Thus it is possible that matters are arranged so that the only piece of information carried by S is that the object recently entering my visual field is red. Further, S has "executive function"; that is, it has a consequence in my behavior. Finally, it has this function in such a way that the "content" of S determines its effect. That is, it is possible that S causes a forearm muscle spasm in virtue of its having the very properties by which it carries the information that the object that has recently moved into my visual field is red.[8]

My objection to the etiological view can now be stated. The features I have just enumerated are all that Dretske requires for saying that S is the belief, about a recently encountered object, that it is red.[9] But in the case I have described it is not reasonable to credit the possessor of S with having the concept of red or, *a fortiori*, with having a belief that something is red. Other people could use the occurrence of the tic as a guide to the presence of red things (once they had discovered the correlation); but the person who has it cannot (as we have set up the case) make any use of it or do any of the things that are expected of people who have the concept of red or beliefs about red things.

If this conclusion is correct, there must be something wrong with Dretske's arguments for his view. There are two such arguments that

8. "When I speak of a semantic structure determining output, I mean that the information . . . constituting the semantic content of that structure is a causal determinant of output. I have already . . . explained what is meant by the information in a structure or signal causing something to happen: viz., information (in signal or structure S) causes E insofar as the properties of S that carry this information are those the possession of which (by S) makes it the cause of E" (198).

9. "To qualify as a cognitive structure, therefore, an internal state must not only *have* a semantic content, it must *be* this content that defines the structure's causal influence on output" (199).

seem to go directly in favor of his view (as opposed to supporting it indirectly, by attempting to rule out alternatives). I shall now state and examine them.

Dretske's first argument for his etiological view begins with a background in which a child is shown robins and bluejays and is encouraged to say "robin" when a robin is present and "not robin" when a bluejay is present (195–196). After she has learned to do this successfully a sparrow appears. The child points to it and *says* "Robin." As Dretske points out, however, it is not immediately clear what the child *believes*. Dretske holds that the belief depends on the semantic content of internal structures that the child developed during training. "If it was this piece of information [that is, *x* is a robin] to which she became selectively sensitive during the training period . . . then the belief she is expressing when she points at the sparrow and says "robin" is a *false* belief. . . . If, on the other hand, the child was (during training) merely responding to the color of the birds, calling those "robin" that were not blue, then the child's belief when it says "robin" while pointing at the sparrow is true" (196). The conclusion that Dretske draws from these observations is that *"what* concept we credit the subject with is a function of *what information* we believe was instrumental in the formation of the relevant internal structure (what *semantic structure* was actually developed)" (195).

Let us flesh this argument out a little. We may begin by giving a name to the relevant internal structure; let us call it "S". S is the state that has the right "forward-looking, functional aspect"; that is, it causally contributes to the child's saying "robin" on the occasion being discussed and contributes to similar bird-related behavior on other occasions. Dretske holds that these causal contributions of S do not determine which concept we ought to assign to it as its meaning or content. What can we add that will determine this? Dretske holds that S becomes established as a regular response in a child because the child's utterances of "robin" are rewarded when, and only when, they follow closely upon certain stimuli (cf. 193).

One possible case is that, in the child's training, S was produced only by stimuli that carried the information that a robin was present. A second possibility is that, in the training period, S was produced only by stimuli that carried the information that a non-blue bird was present. This is a difference that can correspond to the difference in concept possession that we have already seen to be possible. It is the information carried by the stimuli received during the period when S is becoming an established response that Dretske believes to determine both the conceptual content of S and the belief that S's possessor (the child) has.

It would be natural to expect me to give an exposition of Dretske's concept of information at this point. However, it turns out that we do not need to go into the details of that concept in order to see what is wrong with the argument. Instead, let us bring out its structure a little more clearly by further abbreviation. One key premise is that the child who says "robin" may have either of (at least) two beliefs. It does not matter so much which ones they are, so let us just call them "A" and "B". Similarly, the crucial fact about the informational difference in the stimuli is that there is a *difference*. We can mark this by referring to the information I_1 and I_2. Finally, let us use "S is connected with I_n" as a shorthand way of saying that during a child's training period, the structure S occurred only as a result of stimuli that carried the information I_n. Now consider

(1) S is connected with I_1 if and only if the child in whom S occurs has belief A and S is connected with I_2 if and only if the child in whom S occurs has belief B.

If we knew that (1) were true, then it would be reasonable to think that the difference between I_1 and I_2 is what accounts for (or grounds) the difference between the two beliefs. What we must now clearly realize, however, is that Dretske does not argue for (1). He just *says* that, in effect, if S is connected with I_1, the child has one belief and if it's connected with I_2, the child has the other belief.

This comes out very naturally and plausibly because of the way Dretske puts his case, but it amounts simply to begging the question.

Dretske's argument would become stronger, from a formal point of view, if we added the premise that (1) is the *only* way of explaining how the child who looks at the sparrow and says "robin" could have either of two different beliefs. Quite possibly this is what Dretske has in mind. However, merely to assert this point would beg the question against my account and against (CV). More strongly, if we take Dretske's argument this way, it can be undercut by showing how an alternative explanation of the possible difference in beliefs can be provided. I will now show how this can be done.

Let us begin with something common to Dretske's account, my account, and (CV). These views all agree that the conceptual content of S *cannot* be determined *just* by examining S and the utterance (namely "robin") that results from it in the particular case that we are imagining. Thus, they must further agree that the conceptual content of S can be determined only by appealing to something else. The etiologist looks to a certain feature of causes of the structure S on previous occasions. The other views look to consequences that S has had on previous occasions or may have on future occasions. The decisive cases are those in which one would expect different actions, depending on whether the child believes that the sparrow is a robin or believes that the sparrow is a non-blue bird. We can construct such a decisive case by imagining that we tell a child to point to non-blue things, provided they are not just like *this*. As we say "*this*" we point to a robin. Now we lead her to a yard that has a sparrow in it. I will suppose that, as in Dretske's first case, S occurs when she looks at the sparrow. However, because of factors not present during the first exposure to a sparrow (including perhaps, the instruction we have given), the child does not on this occasion say "Robin." There are, of course, other things she can do. Here are two ways in which the scenario we have begun may continue.

(I) S causally contributes to the child's pointing at the sparrow. Here we will probably reason that she does not think that the sparrow is just like the robin we pointed at; that is, she does not think that the sparrow is a robin. This would lead us to assign to S the content "non-blue bird" and to the child the true belief that what she is pointing at is a non-blue bird.

(II) The child does not point to the sparrow. The causal situation is such that she would have done so if S had not occurred. Here we will probably reason that she thinks the sparrow is just like the robin we pointed at. This would lead us to assign to S the content "robin" and to the child the false belief that what she is looking at is a robin.

These alternative developments show how one can account for the differences of belief that a child could have. They do so by reference to possible differences in the consequences of S. Thus they show how non-etiological views can account for the same fact for which Dretske thinks the etiological view is needed.

Two brief comments are in order. (i) Dretske will regard the bits of behavior to which I have pointed as being merely *evidence* for associating different beliefs with S, that is, as evidence upon a matter whose criterion lies in S's etiology (cf. 209). Now, if we had already established the etiological view, this would be a plausible stance to take. We are, however, still discussing an argument for the etiological view. To try to support that argument by premising that the consequences of S described in the preceding paragraph are only evidential and not criterial would clearly be to beg the question. (ii) My example is, of course, a thought experiment. This is especially obvious where we have to imagine that we can tell when S occurs, independently of question-begging assumptions about its causes or effects. This can be no objection, however, because Dretske's view similarly presupposes the intelligibility, in principle, of being able to identify occurrences of the structure S independently of their causes or effects.

I turn now to Dretske's second argument, which comes from a later section of his book titled "The Informational Origin of Concepts". The background of this argument involves the proposal that we might be able to teach someone the concept red without ever exhibiting a red thing. We might use only white things illuminated by red light, while cleverly concealing the abnormality of this situation. In such a case, the subject would never receive the information that something is red—for *information* cannot be false (cf. 45). Thus, if people could acquire the concept red in the way suggested, they could acquire a concept that is not determined by the information contained in any of their internal states. This is contrary to Dretske's view and consequently he must argue against the possibility of acquiring the concept red in the way just imagined.

We must be clear that it is the *concept* red that Dretske thinks cannot be taught without exposure to red things. For, as to the *word* "red", Dretske is prepared to concede that it might be teachable in the imagined way. That is, he takes it upon hypothesis that a subject—whom we may henceforth call "P"—could be trained on white things reflecting red light in such a way as to "blend in with the rest of us" in both normal and abnormal cases involving color discrimination (223). His point is that, even so, P would not possess the concept red. Now, if Dretske could establish this, he would have shown how all the consequences of possessing the concept red could be exhibited by a person who did not have that concept. This result would rule out my account and (CV) and it would be a strong point in favor of the etiological view.

Before turning to Dretske's argument, let us observe that the case he is imagining is truly extraordinary. P is supposed to speak with the rest of us; thus P must be familiar with the facts that things can appear other than they are and that they can do so because of unusual lighting conditions. This is a lot to learn from illusory examples; some may say it is entirely too much. However, rather than argue directly about this, I will proceed to offer a dilemma. Either the word "red" can be learned in the way imagined above or it cannot. If it cannot, it is obvious that Dretske loses a way of arguing for his etiological view. So let us turn our attention to the alternative, that "red" can be learned from white things illuminated with red light, and see where that is supposed to lead us.

Dretske is holding out for the possibility that the concept being used when *P says* "This is red" is a different concept from our concept red. He introduces the label *R* for this concept, whatever it is. We shall follow him in this notation. The question at issue can then be neatly stated as: Is *R* = the concept red? We can represent a portion of Dretske's argument in the following way.

(1) *P*'s concept, *R*, "cannot be the concept *red* if it *correctly* applies to nonred things" (224).
(2) *R* correctly applies to nonred things. Therefore,
(3) *R* is not = the concept red.

Premise (1) seems evident. Premise (2), however, requires and receives further argument. As one would expect, the nonred things to which Dretske thinks *R* correctly applies are the white things used in *P*'s training. Dretske's phrasing leads to a double negative equivalent to (2), that is, the conclusion that these white things are not non-*R*. We can put the argument as follows.

(4) The white things used in *P*'s training could be non-*R* only if "there were criteria for the correct application of *R* that were independent of what the subject was trained to use" (224).
(5) The idea of such independent criteria does not make sense. Therefore,
(6) There are no such criteria. Therefore,
(7) The white things used in *P*'s training are not non-*R*.

Unfortunately for Dretske's case, he is not entitled to assert premise (4). *If* the criteria that P was trained to use do not include anything about correcting for abnormal lighting conditions *then* of course P has not acquired the concept red but at most something like the concept *looks red now*. This concept is indeed a concept under which the white training objects fall. But it is plainly question-begging to assume that the criteria that P was trained to use do not include anything about correcting for abnormal lighting conditions. If we do not assume this, it is open to us to suppose that the criteria of application for R include the requirement that R things must look R under normal conditions. If so, then the white training objects do *not* fall under the concept R, despite the fact that the whole arrangement is so cleverly contrived that P remains mistaken about this. (Presumably any of us who get into P's position all unsuspecting would be mistaken about the color of the training objects also.) Nor is there anything in the least extraordinary about supposing that the criteria for application of R include reference to normal conditions. After all, *ex hypothesi*, P has been taught the correct use of the *word* "red" and so, presumably, would not misclassify things in cases where abnormality of lighting conditions was recognized.

What is truly extraordinary is the idea that a person could learn the whole use of the word "red" from illusory examples alone.[10] My diagnosis of Dretske's argument is that he does not make enough of the extraordinariness of this case at the beginning and then, when it does force itself upon him, he mislocates it as affecting only the acquisition of the concept. But whether this diagnosis is correct or not, I think it is clear that Dretske's second argument has brought us

10. It is, of course, not extraordinary at all for a person to learn the word for a particular shade from a situation containing nothing having that shade. One who was already familiar with the use of color words would surely learn what mauve is from being told that this white thing (which is being viewed in twilight) just now looks to have the color that mauve things actually have. But if we considered this trivial case, Dretske's argument would not even appear to go through.

no closer than the first one did to having a good reason for believing that the etiological view of conceptual content is true.

I turn now to some arguments that are meant to support Dretske's view indirectly, by eliminating alternatives to it. According to the first of these, (CV) must fail because it "founders on the circularity inherent in analyzing the content of our internal states in terms of something (output, response, behavior) that either *lacks* the requisite intentional structure . . . or derives what meaning it has from the meaning of its internal cause" (203). I have, however, given an account of intentionality that does not appeal to thoughts at all. Thus, *if* there are thoughts, I could adopt a consequentialist account of their intentionality without circularity; that is, I could non-circularly assign meanings to thoughts on the basis of utterances and actions of which they were causes.

Dretske would undoubtedly wish to retort that now the circularity must lie in the account of intentionality, which does not appeal to the meanings of thoughts. It is quite clear where he would look for trouble in my account; for he says that "behavior is classifiable as appropriate or inappropriate in relation to the presumed content of those internal states that bring it about" (207). I have, however, gone to some length to show how "behaving like a person who says '*p*'" can be explicated both non-circularly and without appeal to internal states. If my efforts have been successful, I have already answered Dretske's retort.

Two further points are more hinted at than stated by Dretske. Since it is not clear that he puts great weight on them I shall be quite brief. (i) Dretske points out that doorbells do not have beliefs that someone is at the door and would not do so even if we hooked their outputs to tapes that played "Someone is at the door." This observation comes between two claims, each to the effect that the meaningfulness of symbols requires internal states with content (that is, thoughts). (Cf. 204–205). Thus the observation seems intended to be some support for those claims. Such a connection can, however, be undercut by the same considerations that I advanced against the similar claim that words, to be meaningful, must express our mental acts. The fact that doorbells have no thinkings can perfectly well be accounted for without reference to an absence of thoughts; it can be accounted for by that fact that doorbells cannot behave like a person who says "Someone is at the door" (aside from the bare sounding of those words, in the case where the bell is replaced by the playing of a tape).

(ii) Dretske refers to the work of Paul Grice and claims that "our verbal behavior *means* something (in Grice's nonnatural sense of "meaning") because it is an established way of satisfying certain communicative intentions by agents with certain beliefs" (204).[11] He evidently thinks of these intentions and beliefs as thoughts and takes the need for them to support the claim that there are thoughts. This, in turn, is taken to support the etiological view because it would be circular to require intentional thoughts in order to have intentional language *and* require intentional language in order to have intentional thoughts. This whole line of argument, however, is misguided unless there is a refutation of my account of intentionality that is entirely independent of it. For, without such an independent refutation, it is open to me to take Gricean intentions to be thinkings and to apply my general account to this special case. We may consider, for example, an intention that uttering "p" will produce an effect E through recognition of this intention. The people who have this intention will be just those who behave like a person who says "I'm going to produce an effect E through having others recognize that this is what I'm trying to do." No doubt this is a sentence that could be established by (RBU_n) only for some very large n. This is completely consonant, however, with the fact that on

11. Grice's work can be found in "Meaning," *Philosophical Review* 66(1957): 377–388; "Utterer's Meaning and Intentions", *Philosophical Review* 78 (1969): 147–177; and "Utterer's Meaning, Sentence-Meaning, and Word-Meaning", *Foundations of Language* 4 (1968): 225–242.

any construal the establishing of a Gricean intention would be a sophisticated business involving several layers of reflection on language.

The discussion of Dretske's arguments has been necessary and has proved fruitful in clarifying the consequences of both (EV) and my own account. Before going on, however, we should remind ourselves that I began the discussion with a direct argument against Dretske's view. Thus, I am not claiming merely that Dretske has not proved his opponents to be wrong. Instead, the position is that there is a countercase for his view and neither the arguments for the view nor those against alternatives do their job. This leaves us with very good reason to reject the view.

Consequences

In this section I will turn to the main alternative answer to the question "Through what relations might extrinsically intentional thoughts gain their intentionality?" This answer, we recall, is

(CV)   Thoughts derive their intentionality from certain
        features of their effects.

Our discussion of this alternative will depend on a distinction that it has not been necessary to clarify up to this point but that will be of critical importance in this and the next section. It is a distinction between two ways of regarding the role of thoughts in an account of intentionality. One may regard Thoughts as required for Philosophical Analysis or one may regard Thoughts as required by a Causal Hypothesis. This distinction is spelled out as follows.

(TPA)   Intentionality in utterances and thinkings cannot be
         given a satisfactory philosophical account without
         introducing thoughts. Intentionality of utterances and
         thinkings is a logically dependent form of

intentionality, because its existence *entails* the existence of other things having intentionality (that is, thoughts).

(TCH) Intentionality in utterances and thinkings cannot be given a satisfactory causal account without introducing thoughts. Intentionality of utterances and thinkings is *causally* dependent on thoughts. There is no entailment (effects never entail their causes), but no rival causal hypothesis is strong enough to overturn the claim that among the causes of our behavior are internal episodes that can be justifiably said to mean something or be about something.

I shall return to (TCH) in the following section. For the present we are to imagine that we are speaking to people who assert (TPA). Naturally, we will ask them how thoughts have their intentionality. Act theorists will say that thoughts have their intentionality intrinsically; Dretske will say that they get it from the information contained in their causes. These answers, we have seen, have their difficulties, but they at least make *prima facie* sense as answers to the question how thoughts get their intentionality. The key point about (CV), however, is that it does *not* make sense as a further answer to this question. For there is no plausible candidate for the effects from which thoughts might derive their intentionality other than behavior, including utterances. One who asserts (TPA) and also appeals to (CV) is thus caught in a tight circle, deriving intentionality of utterances from intentionality of thoughts, which is derived from intentionality of (among other things) utterances. We can put the point slightly differently. One who works out (CV) will have no plausible alternative to saying that a thought is about what the utterance it causes is about. This presupposes that the utterance is about something; it would hardly make sense to go on to say that the utterance can be about what it is about only because it is produced by a thought that is about that item.[12]

If (TPA) can be successfully supplemented neither with an act view, nor with (EV), nor with (CV), we have good reason to suppose that it is false. This conclusion gives indirect support to the account of Chapter III. Before accepting this conclusion, however, some may seek the strength accruing from standing on two legs instead of one; that is, they may attempt a view that combines (EV) and (CV) and holds that the intentionality of thoughts comes from both their causes and their effects.[13]

There are three comments that I shall make in response to this suggestion. (i) If this view is to be added to (TPA) then, in so far as effects are appealed to, the circularity would still be present. (ii) It seems to me that my countercase for (EV)—the tic in my forearm—has nothing that even comes close to intentionality. If we now imagine that someone teaches me to notice my tic and to respond to it as a sign of the presence of red things, then one may say it has acquired a meaning for me; but then all the work of providing intentionality seems to be on the side of the effects. (iii) The grain of plausibility in the combined view seems to be able to be accounted for in an alternative, natural way. Consider utterances that report current perceptions. It is open to us to say that their meaning derives from their normal effects but to hold also that these normal effects would not remain normal effects unless perceptual reports were generally true when uttered. This, in turn, could hardly be explained without in-

12. This is, of course, a point about which Dretske is perfectly clear. My complaint is that his formulations allow one to slide from attributing circularity to (CV) + (TPA) to attributing it to (CV) by itself, and thence to attributing circularity to any view that resembles (CV) (as my account does) in making the intentionality of an item depend on its consequences.

13. This would be a natural suggestion from those familiar with Wilfrid Sellars' "Some Reflections on Language Games." See his *Science, Perception and Reality* (New York: Humanities Press, 1963).

voking the idea that usually, when a perceptual report is made, the event being reported is causally contributory to the making of the report.

It remains to take up a view in which (CV) is combined with (TCH). The consideration of this view, however, overlaps with the consideration of another view (or set of views) that is currently the focus of much attention. Rather than anticipate some points I shall make, I shall turn directly to this important view and return to (TCH) when a little more background has been provided.

Functionalism

Functionalism, like many views that enjoy wide appeal, is a braid of many strands, not all equally worthy. Our present purposes require us to isolate two of these and to comment upon them. The first strand is the Functionalist Principle, which we discussed in Chapter I:

(FP)   For an organism to be the subject of a mental predicate M is for that organism to perform the function F.

We found this principle unhelpful in Chapter I. However, the predicates with which we were concerned there were of the form "has a sensation of a certain kind". In the meantime we have argued that we ought to expect the treatment of sensations to differ from the treatment of thinkings. Thus we should ask what (FP) leads to when we choose as substituends for "M" the predicates "believes p" or "desires that q (become the case)". The obvious consequence of (FP) is that there is some function that an organism performs if and only if these predicates apply to it. If our first strand of functionalism can be given a defensible development, it must be possible to make good on the idea that there is, at least in principle, a way of specifying this function in a non-circular manner. Now, the account of intentionality I have offered can be regarded as doing exactly this job. Thus, as far as this first strand goes, my view is not only compatible with functionalism but is an instance of it that contains some essential features of its working out.

Let us turn to a second strand in functionalism. This strand is the claim that the proper form for psychology to take involves the postulation of thoughts. Since psychology aims to explain behavior and the typical explanation of a piece of behavior involves having a reason, that is, believing something and desiring something, the typical thoughts that one finds being discussed are beliefs and desires. These are, of course, to be distinguished from believings and desirings. Psychology is supposed to be a science of the *causes* of behavior. Beliefs and desires are, on the functionalist conception we are about to discuss, internal causes of behavior which can be assigned a meaning or content.

This second strand in functionalism is connected with the first in the following way. Beliefs and desires are brain states with meaning. But the meaning that a thing has does not follow from what physical properties it has, for example, how many neurons are involved or how frequently they fire. Instead, the meaning of a brain state is a functional property of it, that is, a property it has in virtue of performing a certain function in the economy of brain states leading to behavior. It should be clear, however, that this second strand is a genuine addition to the first. In the account of intentionality for which I have argued, the first strand is present without any commitment to a causal background of thoughts.

The second strand in functionalism brings us back to the causal hypothesis, (TCH). In this context, (TCH) is naturally allied with the consequentialist view, (CV). For it is a compelling idea that if a brain state has a special role in causing an utterance of p and behavior like that of a person who says "p", and it does not have that special role in causing other utterances or actions, then it should be assigned the meaning p.

So far, I have only tried to clarify the background against which (TCH) appears plausible. I turn now to a discussion of it. The first comment I wish to make is that *strictly speaking* I have no interest in whether (TCH) is true or not. I have given a philosophical account of intentionality. This account is properly opposed to (TPA) and I must therefore argue against that claim. But this is not a book on psychology and I am not obligated to offer a theory of the causes of intentionality. It is enough for me to say what intentionality *is* and what is logically required for it to be had by anything.

I am, however, not content to leave the matter here. The reason is that I fear that some will think that (TCH) is *obvious*—so obvious that no reasonable person could deny it, at least when it is put forth as a general conception without details as to exactly what form the causes of behavior take. The reason this supposition of obviousness is to be feared is that it will make possible a confusion to the effect that there isn't much difference between (TCH) and an analysis of intentionality. It will make possible the mistaken view that we need not worry about the circularity problem, because we do not need behaviorism in any form, because we have a functionalist account of intentionality that we can use in place of behaviorism. To combat these mistakes and confusions, I will argue, not that (TCH) is false, but that it is not obvious, that is, that it could be denied without absurdity. This is sufficient to show that even if (TCH) turns out to be true, it is only a causal fact about intentionality that does not tell us what it is or help us to understand the main problem of how a purely physical thing could have it.

A discussion of the following quotation from Jerry Fodor will enable us to bring out some key points. He writes:

Your standard contemporary cognitive psychologist—your thoroughly modern mentalist—is disposed to reason as follows. To think (e.g.,) that Marvin is melancholy is to represent Marvin in a certain way; viz. as being melancholy (and not, for example, as being maudlin, morose, moody, or merely moping and dyspeptic). But surely we cannot represent Marvin as being melancholy except as we are in some or other relation to a representation of Marvin; and not just to *any* representation of Marvin, but, in particular, to a representation the content of which is *that* Marvin is melancholy, a representation which, as it were, expresses the proposition that Marvin is melancholy. So, a fortiori, at least some mental states/processes are or involve at least some relations to at least some representations.[14]

This passage claims to present a piece of reasoning, yet its key move is so quick as to give us hardly an argument at all. It begins by setting out to tell us what it is to think that Marvin is melancholy. Notice that if our thinking that Marvin is melancholy is *already* conceived as an internal representation, or thought in our regimented sense, then there is *no* reasoning in the second sentence of the quoted passage: that sentence is just a tautology. So let us assume (what seems evident in any case) that the passage means to start with something completely uncontentious—that is, that sometimes we believe that Marvin is melancholy—and move to the conclusion that when cases like this are at hand, there are internal representations. If we ask what justifies this move, we find nothing in the second sentence; representations are introduced as if the need for them was just obvious. The third sentence is no better; "but surely" only reinforces the impression that something is believed to be too obvious to need serious argument. But suppose we do take the need for an argument here seriously? There is just one hint in this passage as to where we might look. It is the fact that Fodor feels it is somehow relevant to mention some of the other things we might have thought about Marvin. When I ask myself why Fodor should be moved to write down these contrasts, the only answer I find is that he must be thinking as follows:

We can think that Marvin is melancholy or that Marvin is

14. See Jerry Fodor, "Methodological Solipsism Considered as a Research Strategy in Cognitive Psychology", reprinted in his *Representations* (Cambridge, Mass.: MIT Press, 1981). The quotation is from p. 225.

maudlin or that Marvin is morose or . . . and so on. Cases of thinking in these ways have a certain similarity—they're all about Marvin—and, of course, certain differences—one is about Marvin's being melancholy, another about his being maudlin, and so on. Now, cases of thinking in these ways have causes. Surely these causes have analogous similarities and differences. They are internal states (brain states) since, after all, behavior is caused by brain states and when we think something about Marvin we are disposed to behave in certain ways. So there must be brain states that are causes of our behavior, which are systematically similar and different in ways that parallel the similarities and differences of the statements (or, to use Fodor's term, propositions) "Marvin is melancholy", "Marvin is maudlin", and so on.

If this really is what is supporting Fodor's story about representations, then we ought to recognize that we do not have good reason for accepting that story. For the line of reasoning just sketched rests on a claim that we may call the Principle of Isomorphism of Causes and Effects:

(PICE) Whenever two effects share a feature, their causes must share an analogous feature.

This principle, however, is unacceptable.[15] For one thing, it implies that a new structure could never arise. Given any structure, (PICE) projects it, so to speak, back onto its cause; but another application of the principle would project the same structure back onto the cause of the cause, and so on *ad infinitum*. This kind of ancestry for structure is clearly not required. For example, my nose is between my eyes, which are between my ears. Surely, this bit of structure is

15. It may appear that I have used this principle myself when I argued in Chapter I that small changes in neural causes should be expected to bring about small changes in qualities of sensations. This, however, is an argument based on considerations of continuity and not on isomorphism of structure.

causally dependent on my genes, but we have no reason to suppose that we can assign genes to body parts in such a way that we can find counterpart relations holding among genes for each relation we find among the body parts. We have no reason to suppose that there is a relation among genes that corresponds in any neat way to the betweenness of nose and eyes, and eyes and ears. We thus have no reason to suppose that the genetic cause of our bodily structure has a structure isomorphic to our bodies.

One might object that genes are not the complete cause of our bodily structure. Our nutritive environment is also a necessary condition for our development. This is, of course, true; but adding the nutritive environment does not give us any reason to suppose that the causes of our structure will be isomorphic to our structure, under some correspondence of genes-plus-nutrients to elements of our structure.

These remarks can be applied to (TCH) as follows. We have good reason to doubt (PICE). If that principle is false, then we should expect that sooner or later in the series of causes stretching back from our utterances, there will be causes that do not have a structure parallel to that of our utterances. Whenever we come to these causes, it will be difficult to treat them as analogous to statements (or propositions). But, lacking direct evidence about the details of the workings of the brain, we really are not in a position to say how many steps back in the causal chain we would have to go to come to causes without a structure that parallels that of our utterances. We do not really know that this situation doesn't happen at the first step back from the effects (that is, our utterances). But if it does happen that soon, (TCH) is false. Thus, we are really not in a position to know that (TCH) is not false.

There is one further argument that might be advanced here, either in conjunction with Fodor's line of thought or independently of it. This argument begins with the idea that reasons cause actions. Further premises are that reasons are composed of beliefs and desires and that brain states are the causes of actions. The conclusion to be drawn from these premises is that brain states can be identified with reasons, that is, with beliefs and desires. So thoughts (beliefs and desires) will be required as causes of actions—required, that is, if we are not to be forced to give up the view (which is surely correct!) that reasons cause actions.[16]

To reply to this line of thought it is necessary and sufficient to exhibit a way of reading "Beliefs and desires cause actions" that has the following two characteristics. (a) It must capture all that we are entitled to by the *common sense* observation that people act for reasons, that is, that they act on the basis of what they believe and what they want. (b) The reading must obviously not imply (TCH). I hope that by this point it will not be difficult to anticipate how such a reading can be given. One could put it several ways: one of them is this. "The causes of believings and desirings are the causes of actions." This really is a truism that gives us no information about the shape of the causes of our actions. When one thinks about the connection between ascribing thinkings and behaving like people who say "p" (cf. (TTA)) it is easy to see that the sentence just quoted comes to about the same as this one: the causes that make us behave like people who say "p" and the causes that make us behave like people who say "q" are sometimes both at work in particular cases, that is, cases in which we behave like people who say both "p" and

16. Both Fodor's idea and this line of argument can be found in a passage from William Lycan, "Psychological Laws", *Philosophical Topics* 12 (1981): 9–38. The passage, which appears on p. 18, runs as follows: "What *kind* of homunctional state might a belief-state be? I take it to be obvious that beliefs have structures of some kind, both on intuitive and on theoretical grounds. Intuitively, because the belief that Donald is intelligent and the belief that Donald is a vegetarian share an element of some kind (either Donald himself or some mental representation of him), as do the belief that Donald is intelligent and the belief that Dan is intelligent; theoretically, because (seemingly) we must suppose Dan's belief that the liquid in front of him is beer and his desire to drink beer share a component if we are to explain their joint function in causing Dan to reach for the liquid in front of him."

"q". The truistic character of this claim is just as it ought to be. Our common sense knowledge of people's motivation does not give us insight into the workings of the brain.

My conclusion from this discussion is that (TCH) is not a triviality, but a genuine causal hypothesis; it is neither a necessary nor an *a priori* truth, but a contingent claim that we have not yet established. This conclusion ought to make it clear that even if (TCH) turns out to be true, it is not part of the philosophical account of intentionality.

CHAPTER V

Self-Consciousness

The proper form of a report of the occurrence of a sensation is "I have such and such a kind of sensation." In Chapter I, I discussed sensations at length but I said very little about *having* sensations or about what is behind the idea that *I* have them. The purpose of the present chapter is to articulate what it is for a person to have a sensation and to respond to a number of objections, conundrums, and confusions surrounding this topic. In the course of doing this I shall be making good on two promissory notes from Chapter I. One of these requires discussion of an argument for adverbialism. The other requires an explanation of how to resist the temptation to introduce awareness of sense-data as an analysis of sensations.

It will shortly be necessary to introduce *feelings* into our discussion. I put these in the same class with sensations, for a reason that by now should sound familiar. It is because we cannot find any way in which brain states could be counted as parts of feelings. There is no way of understanding why a certain ratio of neuron firing frequencies or durations or intensities and so on should compose a feeling of frustration rather than one of elation or fear or pleasant familiarity. We could discover only that one such ratio is correlated with a particular feeling. This would not give us grounds for an identity claim. It would give us good grounds for accepting the view that brain states cause feelings and indeed I think that this is the only reasonable view to take.

I shall occasionally want to make remarks that apply indifferently to all of the non-physical things that I have recognized—that is, sensations, images, and feelings. To do this it will be convenient to have a single term. I thus introduce the technical term "content" to serve this purpose. No particular emphasis will be placed on the question "What contains contents?" However, it does have an answer, namely "People." Contents would naturally appear on a list of all there is that makes up people. The appropriateness of this answer cannot be evident, however, until the end of the following section.

The Unity of the Self

Looking Into Oneself

One's own self is often spoken of as near (as well as dear) and as available to knowledge by the simple activity of introspection or looking into oneself (or one's mind). David Hume is probably the most famous introspector and he has reported his results in the following well-known passage.

> For my part, when I enter most intimately into what I call *myself*, I always stumble on some particular perception or other, of heat or cold, light or shade, love or hatred, pain or pleasure. I never can catch *myself* at any time without a perception, and never can observe any thing but the perception.[1]

Many people, including Hume,[2] have found this passage problematic. Hume's main point, however—that we do not find in introspection any always-present possessor of our "perceptions"—seems to me to be incontestably true. I am thus moved to ask why Hume's passage makes so many think there must be something wrong with

1. David Hume, *A Treatise of Human Nature*, reprinted in C. W. Hendel, Jr., *Hume Selections* (New York: Scribner's, 1927), p. 84. Parenthetical references in this section are to pages of this edition.
2. See Appendix to Book I of Hume's *Treatise*, pp. 103–106.

it. There are two facts about what I find when I look into myself that Hume does not mention and that seem to provide the answer.

Some of our feelings are quite definite, like the feeling that goes with extreme frustration or the feeling that one has after suddenly being frightened and then realizing there is actually no danger. Other feelings are more elusive. One such feeling is the feeling of comfortable familiarity. We do not always have such a feeling when we are in comfortable and familiar surroundings, but sometimes the familiar does feel familiar. Another is the feeling of knowing where we are or where our destinations lie when we are relying on our "sense of direction". We do not have such a feeling all the time that we know where we are but we can have it, and we can contrast that feeling with what it feels like to be lost or what it feels like to come upon something from an unexpected angle and realize that we have been disoriented for some time. Among the elusive feelings is one that seems to lie behind our sense of ourselves. This is the feeling that we can connect our contents with our context. By this I mean the feeling that if we were asked what sensations immediately preceded any we are now having, we could answer correctly; that if we are having an image of a past action, we could say what came before and after it, why we did it, and how people reacted to it. We feel that we could give reasons for assertions made in our inner speech and explain why we happen to be silently soliloquizing about whatever topic it is that we are concerned with.[3] I am not saying that this

3. Hume seems to have come close to recognizing the feeling I am talking about when he wrote, "We only *feel* a connection or determination of the thought, to pass from one object to another. It follows, therefore, that the thought alone finds personal identity, when reflecting on the train of past perceptions, that compose a mind, the ideas of them are felt to be connected together, and naturally introduce each other" (106). However, the feeling Hume describes here differs from the one to which I am calling attention in two respects. First, the former is a feeling of the passage of particular perceptions, while the latter is a feeling that one can go on in many directions, without any particular direction for going on having yet been suggested. Second, the former is a feeling of the naturalness of the *passage* of perceptions, while the latter is a feeling that can be contained within one complex (but not temporally complex) content.

feeling is an infallible guide to what we can in fact do; and I am not suggesting that we have this feeling at all the times that we actually know our way around in the connections of our contents with their causes, predecessors, and successors. We can, however, have such a feeling and we are particularly likely to have it when we are asking ourselves about the connectedness of our contents with each other and with our behavior. This feeling is nothing but a "particular perception" that we sometimes find, but it is one that has a special relevance to the idea of a self that is the same self throughout a succession of different contents. Natural descriptions of this feeling imply that there is some whole that includes present contents but also includes something else, namely, causes of my being able to go on and make connections in the way that I feel I can.

The second addition we must make to Hume's introspective report is this. He speaks of "perceptions" as if they occurred one by one. He compares the mind to a theatre where "several perceptions *successively* make their appearance" (85; emphasis added). In actual fact, however, when we look into ourselves we find something complex. We have, all at once, a sensation, for example, or perhaps several of them; maybe some definite feelings or some bit of inner monologue and perhaps some elusive feelings as well. These come together and when we remember a case of looking into ourselves we remember these as coming together. What we actually find when we look within is thus not "particular perceptions", if this means single contents, but rather complex contents.

It might be thought that it is arbitrary, and therefore of trivial moment, whether we view our contents as one complex or as several (perhaps simultaneous) elements. We owe to Kant, however, the clear recognition that this is not so. We may phrase one of Kant's insights this way: A plurality of awarenesses is not the same as an awareness of plurality.[4] What I know about introspection is not ade-

4. See *Immanuel Kant's Critique of Pure Reason*, tr. N. K. Smith (London: Macmillan, 1961): "If we were not conscious that what we think is the same as what we thought a moment before, all reproduction in the series of representations would be

quately reflected by saying, for example, that I have looked within and found a pain and also I have looked within and found myself inwardly expressing the wish that I didn't have to teach today. We could put what is missing from this description in a contentious way that would appear to be in conflict with Hume's denial that we find a self in introspection. That is, we could say that we have sometimes known—and known by looking within—that it is the same "I" who has the pain and who wishes for relief from having to teach. What we ought to say, however, is that what we find when we look within are complexes in which there can co-occur sensations, feelings, and images—for example, a pain and auditory images of the words "I wish I didn't have to teach today."

In ordinary situations the elements in our complex contents have something to do with each other. Our internal monologue, for example, may be about something that is in our memory image. Again, a memory image of a scene in which I previously had a sensation may come into a complex that includes an occurrence of a sensation of the same kind. There must, of course, be causes of this relatedness of our contents but, unlike the contents themselves, these causes are not what we find by looking within. Nor do we know very much about these causes by any other means. There is the further complication that, since we can report on our complexes, their causes are also causally connected to our ability to speak. The epiphenomenalistic structure detailed in Chapter I was stated as it applies to single sensations but it applies *mutatis mutandis* for complexes. The causal complexity required by all these connections is quite marvelous. Some may think it a bit too marvelous and thus may doubt the view that requires it. However, such causal complex-

useless. For it would in its present state be a new representation which would not in any way belong to the act whereby it was to be gradually generated. The manifold of representation would never, therefore, form a whole" (A ed., 134). "Combination does not, however, lie in the objects" (B ed., 154). "But the combination of a manifold in general can never come to us through the senses" (B ed., 151). See also the first paragraph of sec. 17 of the B edition deduction, pp. 155–156.

ity is not peculiar to epiphenomenalism; it is required by any adequate view. Even on, say, an identity theory there would have to be some causal account of why related events come together, how it is that they compose a complex, and how they are causally related to our ability to report on them.

Reports are, of course, only one form of behavior to which the causes of our contents are causally connected. The causes of our pains, for example, also cause us to withdraw our injured parts. The causes of resolutions for the future, made in inner speech, cause memories and further inner speech as the time for action approaches. Ultimately, they may make their contribution to the action that was resolved upon. When we buy some hamburger, unwrap it before depositing it in the frying pan, cook it, and then eat it, we may have some contents relating to hamburgers. It is clear, however, that there are causes that keep this whole performance together, which we do not know by introspection. These causes are, presumably, also the causes of those relatively few contents relating to hamburgers that we do have.

The foregoing observations suggest that there are two kinds of unity that people have. On the one hand, there is the unity that appears to us when we look within. This consists of the feeling that we can go on indefinitely in relating present contents to our memories and our plans and of the fact that our contents are almost always complex. We might call this "apparent unity" because it appears to us; but that might suggest that it is illusory, which is not at all the point. So let us call it "internal unity" to remind ourselves that it is what we find by looking within. By contrast, we may call "external" the unity that, though it is obvious enough, is not something we come upon by introspection. This unity consists in our being so organized that our firm intentions get carried out into real actions, that we don't forget what we are doing in the middle of a job, that the causes of our sensations cause correct sensation reports, and so on.

Having Contents

In this section I will begin the discussion of the following Condition for the Having of Contents.

(CHC)   A person S has a content c just in case c is a content and is directly caused by some change in or condition of S's body.

I believe this condition to be the correct one. However, I expect the conviction that it is correct to grow only slowly, as we see that (CHC) holds up in the face of objections and that alternatives only multiply our problems without increasing our understanding. The remarks immediately below clarify and point out some advantages of (CHC).

It is obvious that contents cannot be made to be contents by being brought into a relation to something else. That is, we have no way of making sense of the notion that a pain or an afterimage or a feeling could have been not a pain, afterimage, or feeling and then have become so because something else came into existence or because it was brought into a relation to something else. One virtue of (CHC) is that it cannot be misread as an attempt to say what it is that makes a thing a content (since "c is a content" occurs on its right side). It is clear that its job is *solely* to say which contents belong to which people. When this job is not confused with any other one I think it will be obvious that the causal connection in (CHC) will suffice for its performance.

If I hit you on the head and cause you to "see stars" then the changes in my body that brought about my hitting you contribute causally to the sensation. Yet it is your sensation and not mine. This observation will explain the point of the word "directly" in (CHC). Any bodily cause, b of a content, c is to be counted as *directly* causing c just in case there are no causes in the process leading from b to c that involve parts of a body other than the one in which b occurs.

A change in my body at t_1 could cause, let us say, c_1 while a change in my body at t_2 could cause c_2. This much does not ensure that c_1 and c_2 are parts of one complex content. Nor does it ensure that memories of c_1 and c_2 or inner speech about them ever occur as parts of the same complex. This might lead someone to observe that (CHC) does not account for the unity of the self and to complain about it for that reason. The observation is correct but the complaint is unjustified. (CHC) is not meant to account for the unity of the self; it is only a condition for determining which contents go with which people.

(CHC) yields an answer to the question "Whose content is c?" only if we can tell who it is whose bodily changes caused c. This can be problematic. Suppose, for example, that Jones' brain is transplanted into the body of an unknown victim of a brain tumor. We shall call this recipient body "Body A". Next, Smith's brain is transplanted into the body that until recently housed the brain that is now in the cranium of Body A. Let us call this body "Body B". After everyone has healed up we might be uncertain whether we should say (a) "Jones has a new brain" (and point at Body B when asked to point out Jones) or (b) "Jones has a new body" (and point at Body A when asked to point out Jones). If so, we will also be uncertain whether or not the contents that are caused by events in the brain in the cranium of Body B belong to Jones. This fact, however, is no objection to (CHC). That condition is not meant to be a condition for determining who is who. Once we know who Jones is (however we come to know that) we will be able to use (CHC) to assign contents correctly. This is all that (CHC) is intended to do (and all that needs to be required of it).

Some may think that what I have just said is not sufficient. The reason is that it is plausible to think that part of the resolution of who Jones is should depend on who has access to Jones' memories. But memory images and inner speech that goes with remembering are contents. Thus, it is plausible to think that contents must be assigned in order to decide who Jones is and therefore before it has been decided who Jones is. If this is plausible it must at least be intelligible; but, according to the previous paragraph, if (CHC) is asserted this is not intelligible. Thus (CHC) must be wrong.

The last paragraph but one is, however, not really in conflict with the idea that we ought to call Body A "Jones" because the person whose body it is possesses Jones' memories. There are two relevant points. First, it will be from Body A's mouth, and from this mouth only, that reports will issue that generally give the truth about things in the past that only the then-possessor of Body B witnessed. Second, it is a very plausible assumption that the brain is the most important causal factor in the production of contents. Thus it is natural to suppose that the contents caused later by the brain in Body A will be very like those caused earlier by the brain in Body B (that is, the same brain before the transplant). Since some of what is involved in memory is contents (images, inner speech) this would imply a continuity of the memories of the later person having Body A with those of the earlier person having Body B. This is sufficient to account for the plausibility of the line sketched in the preceding paragraph.[5]

Objections and Alternatives

Michael Levin's Monadic Thesis

I have said that when we look within we find that our contents are complex. I have not, however, argued that this is a necessary truth. As far as anything I have said goes, it would be possible for a single content to occur just by itself. We can even imagine making a

---

5. The argument here does not require one to say that the points mentioned would be decisive in settling who Jones is. We need only make the appeal to continuity of memory plausible (and therefore intelligible).

human body (or something physically indistinguishable from a human body), letting it have one non-complex content, and then destroying it—so that the entire history of this "person's" contents is, say, one moment of ecstatic feeling. No doubt this is, causally speaking, a very extraordinary case. But since any content can occur without any particular other one, their causes are only contingently related. While it does not logically follow from this that one can produce a content without there being *any* surrounding complex, I know of nothing that would rule out this possibility.

This possibility suggests another. Perhaps a brain state is a sufficient cause of an ecstatic feeling; perhaps even a part of a brain being in a certain state will be a sufficient cause of it. So let us suppose we make something that is physically indistinguishable from a part of a brain.[6] We so construct this that when it is finished it is in the state that causes an ecstatic feeling. We may suppose that when we make just this part it is small enough so that no other content is caused. We destroy our creation a moment after we have finished it. Now, an ecstatic feeling has existed. But an attempt to apply (CHC) will not yield a person who has the feeling. This is, of course, no objection to (CHC) because it is clear on independent grounds that there is no person who has the ecstatic feeling. That is, the only plausible candidates for what might "have" the ecstatic feeling are the brain part that causes it, and the whole composed of this brain part together with the feeling. Neither of these, however, is a person.

I believe the foregoing to be a genuine logical possibility (although maybe it is not a genuine physical possibility). However, it

6. One should not think of a *chunk* of brain-matter here but rather of a few neural cells arranged in a three-dimensional net, with their synapses and just enough supporting tissue to preserve the spatial arrangement.

Some of the reflections in this section were occasioned by Roland Puccetti, "The Refutation of Materialism", *Canadian Journal of Philosophy* 8 (1978):157–162. My conclusions, however, diverge from Puccetti's.

certainly sounds objectionable at first blush to allow for a feeling with no one to feel it. There is, in fact, an articulate objection to this idea in the work of Michael Levin.[7] Levin's argument is interesting and would repay examination from several points of view. My discussion of it here will be guided by two considerations. First, I must show that it does not really rule out the possibility of a case that the view presented thus far in this chapter implies to be possible. Second, Levin's argument is part of a defense of a form of adverbialism. In Chapter I, I deferred consideration of this defense. Now, in showing that the argument does not go through, I shall be showing that there is no need to revise the position I took in Chapter I.

According to Levin, a view of sensations of the kind I have proposed "prompts the materialist to argue that after-images are virtual, that statements about after-images ascribe the monadic predicate 'x has a yellow after-image' (or 'x is yellow after-imaging'). If this thesis is true, there need be nothing yellow when someone has a yellow after-image" (92). In contrast, I have maintained that "x has a yellow after-image" asserts a relation to hold between a person, x and an individual yellow afterimage.

Levin calls the view expressed in the above quotation "the monadic thesis". Many authors have been attracted to this thesis because of the alleged benefits it confers. Levin, however, is unusually clear about the need to have a direct argument for it. The argument he gives turns upon "the familiar observation that there cannot conceivably be an unexperienced pain" (94). Levin speaks of pain here because he takes this example as "our stalking horse for psychological ascriptions generally" (103). The introduction of this example inevitably raises the question whether pain really is an appropriate stalking horse; that is, whether an argument stated for after-images would bring out something more clearly than its approximate corre-

7. Michael Levin, *Metaphysics and the Mind-Body Problem* (Oxford: Oxford University Press, 1979), pp. 92–97. Parenthetical numbers in this subsection refer to pages of this book.

sponding argument stated in the idiom of pains, or conversely. I believe that in fact the choice of example makes no significant difference. However, the only way I know of to be convincing about this point is to state crucial parts of the argument and my discussion if it in versions appropriate to each example. I will begin with a formulation appropriate to the pain example.

(A)   If "x is in pain" has genuinely relational form (so that it is perspiciously represented by, say, "$I(x,y)$"[8]) then it is possible that a pain occur without there being anyone who is in (that) pain (that is, $\Diamond(\exists y)[y$ is a pain & $\sim(\exists x)I(x,y)])$.

This is an instance of what Levin calls "Hume's law", that is, the claim that there can be no necessary connections among distinct or merely externally related things. Now, the "familiar observation" that pains must be experienced can be expressed as

(B)   It is not possible that a pain occur without there being someone who is in (that) pain (that is, $\sim\Diamond(\exists y)[y$ is a pain & $\sim(\exists x)I(x,y)])$.

Modus tollens then gives

(C)   "x is in pain" does not have genuinely relational form.

But "x is in pain" says *something* about x and if not a relational something then a predicative or monadic something, representable by, for example, "x hurts."

Restated so as to apply to afterimages, this argument becomes:

(A′) If "x has a yellow afterimage" has genuinely relational form (for example, $(\exists y)[Ay$ & Yy & $H(x,y)])$ then it is

8. Levin uses the notation "$P(x,y)$" but this suggests that the view being criticized holds pain to be a relation rather than a property of an item that may be related to a person. Neither my view nor the view to which Levin directs his critique holds this. I have therefore chosen a notation that avoids this suggestion.

possible that a yellow afterimage occur without there being anyone who has it (that is, $\Diamond(\exists y)[Ay \ \& \ Yy \ \& \ \sim(\exists x)H(x,y)]$).

(B') It is not possible that a yellow afterimage occur without there being someone who has it (that is, $\sim\Diamond(\exists y)[Ay \ \& \ Yy \ \& \ \sim(\exists x)H(x,y)]$). Therefore,

(C') "x has a yellow afterimage" does not have genuinely relational form.

When we try to put this conclusion positively we find a small difference from the previous case. To rephrase "x is in pain" in such a way as to give it a monadic ring, we had only to use the readily available "x hurts." To make the analogous move in the present case, however, we have to make special contrivance and say either "x is in a yellow-afterimaging state" or "x afterimages yellowly."

These arguments are both unsound, and they are so for the same reason: their second premises are false. It will be convenient to show this by using materials available in Levin's own view. Levin allows for awarenesses of pains, though, of course, these are understood non-relationally. There being no pains properly speaking, according to Levin, they are not identified with anything. But awarenesses of pains *are* identified with something, namely, brain states. Now if you are inclined to accept (B) you will probably be inclined to accept the idea that there couldn't be an awareness of pain that isn't *someone's* awareness of pain. But *this cannot be right*. All you have to do to see this is to imagine excising a portion of a brain just big enough to contain the parts that are required for producing a state that is (identical with) an awareness of pain. This may, of course, be beyond the capabilities of neurosurgery, but it is not logically impossible. Now, if the person from whom you've excised this brain-part isn't quite dead, kill him or her. Then take the brain-part and produce in it the state that is a pain awareness. Now you will have a pain awareness that cannot plausibly be supposed to be anyone's awareness.

I have used some of Levin's own views for convenience and also to make it evident that I am not begging a question against him. But the point is not an *ad hominem*. You get the same argument if you are a dualist, as we have seen. You get it just so long as you say that there are brain states that are the sufficient causes of awarenesses of pains, or that are sufficient causes of pains. Boiled down to its bare bones the argument is that a pain is not a person. Thus the cause of a pain is not the cause of a person. By Hume's law it is logically possible for the cause of a pain to occur (and thus, of course, to bring about a pain) without the cause of a person occurring (and thus without there being a person to have the pain).

This result may tempt some people to adopt the view that it is, after all, logically impossible to cause a pain to come into existence without also causing the existence of a person who has the pain. This, however, is a most unpromising move. To see why let us note that distinct sensations can occur separately and thus have distinct causes. Now let P_1 be the person whose existence is a necessary consequence of the existence of one sensation, say, a pain and let P_2 be the person whose existence is a necessary consequence of the existence of, say, a yellow afterimage. Since I can bring about the pain without the afterimage, or vice versa, either of P_1 and P_2 can exist without the other. Therefore P_1 and P_2 are different persons. This argument works for any pair of distinct sensations. Thus, the person who has one sensation will always be distinct from the person who has a different sensation; that is, it will be impossible for the same person to have more than one sensation. This, however, is plainly in conflict with our concept of a person.

Although (B) and (B') are false, there is a strong intuition that seems to support them. Our rejection of Levin's argument cannot be really convincing until we have articulated that intuition correctly and shown that the monadic thesis does not follow from such a correct articulation together with Hume's law. There are in fact two claims that seem to be true, evident, and likely to be confused, on occasion, with (B). These are

(B_1) It is not possible that people have pains that they do not feel (or of which they are not aware); and

(B_2) A pain is a feeling (or kind of awareness); it is thus not possible that a pain occur without there occurring a feeling (or kind of awareness).

Levin asserts (B_2) and gives us no reason to think he would deny (B_1). Thus we can move immediately to the important question, whether the thrust of Levin's original argument can be reconstructed around these revised candidates for the second premise.

If we wish to derive (C) from (B_1) by modus tollens, then our other premise must read:

(A_1) If "x is in pain" has genuinely relational form, then it is possible that people have pains that they do not feel.

(A_1), however, is false. To see this we must first observe that the move from x's having an F to x's feeling an F is trivially available whenever F is a feeling. The availability of this move is partially constitutive of our concept of a feeling. Further, that pain is a feeling (which, let us note, is what (B_2) says) is partially constitutive of our concept of pain. So, of course, we have no place in our conceptual framework for people having pains that they do not feel. Now, this little explanation has made no claim one way or another about the logical form of "x is in pain", and so there is no reason to suppose that if "x is in pain" has genuinely relational form we are going to have to give up the idea that "x has a pain" is logically related to "x feels a pain." But if this is correct, the implication asserted by (A_1) does not hold and (A_1) is false.

If we wish to get (C) from (B_2) by modus tollens, then our other premise must read:

(A_2) If "x is in pain" has genuinely relational form, then it is possible that a pain occur without there occurring a feeling (or kind of awareness), that is, possible that a pain occur that is not a feeling.

Formally, this is no more plausible than "If 'x owns a cow' has genuinely relational form then it is possible that a cow exist without there existing an animal, that is, possible that a cow exist that is not an animal." The only way to account for someone's even suspecting that the antecedent of (A_2) is relevant to its consequent is to imagine it being supposed that a feeling cannot exist without being some-body's feeling. But this supposition takes us back to ground already covered. The cause of a feeling need not cause anything that is not logically inseparable from a feeling; and a person cannot be held to be logically inseparable from a feeling unless one countenances as many persons as there are feelings.

The case for afterimages parallels the case for pains. The true and evident replacements for (B′) are:

(B′$_1$) It is not possible that people have yellow afterimages of which they are not visually aware; and

(B′$_2$) A yellow afterimage *is* a (certain kind of) visual awareness; it is thus not possible that a yellow afterimage occur without there occurring a (certain kind of) visual awareness.

"Visual awareness" is not quite the ordinary term that "feeling" is; indeed, to some extent its conceptual connections have been explicitly modeled on those of terms like "feeling" rather than being merely found in ordinary use. But the connections are there, and parallel to those of "feeling"; and they are firmly rooted in such ordinary phrases and remarks as "seeing stars" and "He got so drunk he started seeing things." The term "visual awareness" can in fact be regarded as a device for capturing the point of such remarks without confronting the ambiguities of the verb "to see" at every turn.

As replacements for premise (A) we have:

(A′$_1$) If "x has a yellow afterimage" has genuinely relational form then it is possible that people have yellow afterimages of which they are not visually aware; and

(A′₂)   If "x has a yellow afterimage" has genuinely relational form then it is possible that a yellow afterimage occur without there occurring a (certain kind of) visual awareness, that is, possible that a yellow afterimage occur that is not a (certain kind of) visual awareness.

As before, the point is that the reasons why the replacements for premise (B) are true have nothing to do with assumptions about the logical form of "x has a yellow afterimage"; therefore no particular assumption about that form implies the contradictory of either replacement for (B); and therefore the replacements for premise (A), which assert such implications, are false.

I conclude that Levin's argument for the monadic thesis is unsound. It cannot be restored to soundness by replacing the faulty second premise by similar-sounding truths, for preserving validity then requires revised versions of the first premise that are false. This conclusion has two consequences. First, it turns aside Levin's defense of adverbialism. Thus we are entitled to reaffirm our discussion in Chapter I, which depended in part on rejecting that view. Second, we have shown how it is acceptable to hold that pains without persons are logically possible. The fact that this is a consequence of the view set out above is thus no objection to that view.

Doubts About Complexes

The argument of the preceding section rests on the premise that sensations are independent of one another. The emphasis placed on this fact may cause one to wonder whether, or how, independent sensations can be parts of a complex. Doubts here may grow into doubts about my account of the unity of the self and ultimately into an objection to that account, in so far as it makes use of complexes.

To forestall such an objection I shall give a more detailed discussion of complexes than has been required up to this point.

We have already made use of the fact that the causes of independent sensations may occur independently of one another. To this we may add the following principle: the causes that bring about a sensation when it occurs by itself are also at work when it occurs as part of a complex. This is not a necessary truth, but it would seem perverse to deny it unless one had clear empirical grounds to do so and these are lacking. Such a denial would also force the question whether the cause of a sensation had to be different each time it occurred in a complex with different other parts. By way of illustration of the principle, suppose that a burn on my finger causes a pain and that it does so by causing a certain neural firing, G_1 in my brain. Suppose I look at a bright light and then close my eyes, so that I come to have an afterimage; that is to say, I now have a complex content that includes the same kind of pain and an afterimage. It is overwhelmingly plausible to think that G_1 is still at work and is what is causing my complex content to include a pain.

Let us suppose that if there had been no pain my afterimage would have been caused through the production of the neural firing, G_2. Naturally it is extremely plausible to say that when the pain is also present, G_2 is still at work and is responsible for the fact that my content includes an afterimage. Shall we say, then, that the cause of my complex content is *just* G_1 and G_2? Well, we would obviously have to understand that these were occurring at the same time. We would also have to understand that G_1 and G_2 are not merely neural firing *types*, which might be instantiated in different bodies. Rather, they must be individuals in the same body. Is this sufficient to guarantee the occurrence of a complex sensation? It seems possible that it is not. Psychological case studies have made extraordinary dissociations familiar. One "personality" can know nothing of what has happened to another one for several years. We are not in a position to rule out the possibility of dissociation going so deep that events in the same body at the same time cause a pain and an after-image, but no complex sensation. In such a case the pain might be felt by one personality while the afterimage was had by a different one.

Dissociation has its causes. Likewise the occurrence of a complex will have a cause. If we put this together with the idea that the same causes of sensations are at work when those sensations occur by themselves and when they occur as parts of various complexes we get the following view. There is some relation R (presumably, being neurally connected in some way) such that when, for example, G_1 and G_2 stand in that relation there occurs a complex sensation; whereas if G_1 and G_2 were to occur without standing in R there would be two sensations but they would not be parts of the same complex sensation. In normal people, causes like G_1 and G_2 stand in R whenever they occur at the same time, but perhaps in dissociative cases simultaneity of occurrence in the same body is not sufficient to ensure that R holds.

There are two directions in which this view needs to be amplified. The first concerns (CHC). One may be tempted to think that this must be given up and replaced by some more complex condition according to which the assignment of sensations to the same person would depend on their causes standing in the relation R. I resist this move for two reasons. First, (CHC) is not intended to yield an analysis of what it means for sensations to be parts of the same complex. It will tell you at most when two sensations are had by the same person. These two tasks are easily confused because in normal people simultaneous causes of sensations stand in R. But the foregoing discussion shows how the predicate "sensations had simultaneously by the same person" is logically distinct from the predicate "sensations that are parts of the same complex". Second, the several "personalities" in a split-personality case all belong in some sense to one person—the same who is said to be suffering and to be in need of help. We say, for example, "Sybil had many personalities" and there is nothing objectionable about this way of expressing ourselves.[9] Thus, while we *could* proceed differently, it is unobjectionable to continue to affirm (CHC) as the criterion for assigning contents to persons. We may, whenever it is germane, add that simultaneous sensations that (CHC) assigns to the same person will not be parts of the same complex if their causes are not connected by the relation R.

The second point that requires further comment is this. The relation R is part of what is needed to cause a complex content but it cannot, of course, be any part of the effect to which it causally contributes. This observation may lead one to ask what the analysis of the effect is, that is, what the analysis of a complex content is, or what the difference is between a pain by itself and a pain in a complex. Now these questions have simple answers that are entirely correct and completely adequate. To wit: A complex content is one that has parts. Parts of a complex may stand in many relations to each other. They occur simultaneously and they may differ or resemble in intensity and in color, shape, pitch, odor, flavor, warmth, and so on. But none of these relations "make" the items they relate to be co-constituents of a complex. What makes sensations co-constituents of a complex, in the straightforward causal sense of "making", is their causes standing in the relation R. What "makes" sensations co-constituents of a complex, in the sense of an analysis of what a complex *is,* is that they are parts of the same complex. There is no other sense of "making" that has application here.

Although what I have just said is in fact adequate, it is apt not to appear to be so. The two observations that follow are intended to help relieve this misplaced sense of inadequacy. The first one is this. Some complex sensations are not much different from some sensations that would ordinarily be thought of as simple. Consider a sensation that would naturally be described as a complex whose parts are two white squares, close together. This could be thought of

9. See F. R. Schreiber, *Sybil* (Chicago: Regnery, 1973).

as actually something *less* than a single sensation of a white rectangle, in the way that Figure 3(*e*) is Figure 3(*a*) with a piece missing. One could regard 3(*e*) as introducing division into a field that is already there in 3(*a*). We may also note that one could very gradually transform 3(*a*) into 3(*e*) by passing through such intermediate stages as 3(*b*)–3(*d*). From this point of view, the interesting fact about sensations is not that they can contain parts, but that even in a case like 3(*a*) they involve fields, that is, they involve qualities that are "spread out" over an area that already contains the potential for division.

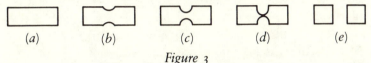

| (*a*) | (*b*) | (*c*) | (*d*) | (*e*) |

Figure 3

The second observation concerns a misleading picture. A pain can occur with any number of things or by itself. If I ask you to imagine a pain, there would be no reason to imagine anything else in particular along with it and so you will probably think of a case of a simple content where there is nothing but the pain. Likewise, if I ask you to imagine an afterimage you will probably imagine a simple content. Now, if I ask you to tell me what it takes to make two sensations (for example, a pain and an afterimage) to be parts of a complex, you may think of a case of a pain occurring by itself and an afterimage occurring by itself and ask yourself what you have to add to those to get a complex sensation. This will quite naturally strike you as a deep, not to say insoluble, problem. In fact, however, it is not a problem but just a mistaken formulation stemming from a bad picture. It is just as if, when asked to think of a large square, one imagined a square with nothing inside it, and when asked to think of a small circle, one imagined a circle with nothing around it. If one were then asked how there could be a figure of a square with a small circle inscribed in it, one might get to feeling stumped—because, of course, there is nothing one can *add to* an empty square and an unsurrounded circle to get a circle inscribed in a square. But all this should have no tendency at all to make us think that there is any problem in there being a complex figure of the kind indicated.

Moorean Awarenesses

In the first part of this chapter, I distinguished two kinds of unity of the self. In accounting for these kinds of unity, I referred only to facts about contents and facts about their causes. There is no further kind of individual thing that is required by my analysis of the self. Some philosophers will think that this account leaves something out, namely, an awareness that is allegedly required as something to be aware of contents. G. E. Moore's influential statement of this view is clear and the relevant points needed in defense of the view I have presented can be brought out in response to it. The key argument is as follows:

> We all know that the sensation of blue differs from that of green. But it is plain that if both are *sensations* they also have some point in common. . . .
> I will call the common element 'consciousness'. . . .
> We have then in every sensation two distinct elements, one which I call consciousness, and another which I call the object of consciousness. . . .[B]lue is one object of sensation and green is another, and consciousness, which both sensations have in common, is different from either (17).[10]

Moore goes on to rename this common element "awareness" and to claim that

> a sensation is, in reality, a case of 'knowing' or 'being aware of' or 'experiencing' something. When we know that a sensation

10. G. E. Moore, *Philosophical Studies*, first published in 1922. Parenthetical references in this subsection are to the edition of Littlefield, Adams & Co., Totowa, N. J., 1965.

of blue exists, the fact that we know is that there exists an awareness of blue. And this awareness is not merely, as we have hitherto seen it must be, itself something distinct and unique, utterly different from blue: it also has a perfectly distinct and unique relation to blue. . . . This relation is just that which we mean in every case by 'knowing' (24–25).

It is easy to criticize the consequences of this view. For example, a sensation is held to involve a relation to *blue*, not to a blue individual. Thus the apparent individuality of sensations is unaccounted for. Further, it appears that knowing a sensation of blue is knowing a knowing of blue. But I can have such a knowing in one way—that is, I can know that I know what blue is—without knowing a sensation of blue. Further, we are entitled to ask what this element called "an awareness" is. Moore tells us that awarenesses are "extremely difficult to fix", "transparent" (20), and "as if [they] were diaphanous" (25). This is very fishy, especially as it is supposed to be easy to tell which items are sensations and the only way we have of doing this according to Moore's account is to know that they have the common awareness elements. Finally, Moore holds that awarenesses and blue, green, and so on are only externally related. This has the consequence that an awareness could exist without being related to anything, that is, without being the awareness of anything. This consequence, however, is unintelligible.

There is a task that is much more important than the elaboration of these criticisms. This is to see clearly what is wrong with the initial argument, which seems to compel one into the mistaken view. The easiest way to bring out the fallaciousness of the argument is to consider the following parallel.

We all know that an area of blue differs from an area of green. But it is plain that if both are *areas* they also have some point in common. . . .

I will call the common element "patchness". . . .

We have then in every area two distinct elements, one which I call patchness, and another which I call the object of patchness.

If "patchness" remained a term for a quality, this would be less problematic than it is. But "consciousness", after renaming as "awareness", becomes a term for individuals. Thus Moore speaks of "an awareness" and "this awareness". The analogous move for our parallel is to treat "patchness" as equivalent to "patch". When we do this, we get the absurd view that *in* every area there are two distinct elements, a patch and some color. The problem with this is that either the patch is colored or it is not. If it is not, we have to admit that there are colorless patches. This seems not so much like an hypothesis as an inadvertent mistake that no one would seriously intend. But if the patch is colored, then it is false that there are *two* things in an area. In having a colored patch, we have all that we need for a colored area. It is mere redundancy to tack on "and some color."

It is easy to see what it is in Moore's text that leads him into error. It is the move from "something in common" to "a common element". The former could very well be a quality or a relation; the latter strongly suggests a common type of individual. One is not entitled to the inference from one to the other. To make this clear, consider that Socrates and an ass have "something in common", namely that they're both animals. One is certainly not entitled to conclude that there is an Animal that is a constituent of each one, nor that there is some kind of animal-making part of which Socrates and the ass must each contain one. Areas also have a generic kind of commonness; that is, being bluely colored is one way of being an area (or, one species of area) and being greenly colored is another. This is how things also stand with contents. "Content" is a generic term, of which "sensation", "image", and "feeling" are species. Under the first of these we have the subspecies pain, afterimages, ringings in the ears, and so on. Under these we have such ultimate species as throbbing pain in the toe, yellow oval afterimage, and G♯ ringing in the ears. There are, of course, many individuals of each species.

Noticings

Noticings of colors, sounds, tastes, and so on, were introduced in Chapter I and were counted as sensations on the strength of their similarity to the afterimages, ringings in the ears, and aftertastes that were taken to be paradigms of sensations. The themes of Chapter I concerned what holds of sensations generally and there was no reason to single out noticings for special consideration. In the present context, however, there may be some temptation to introduce a distinction between the noticed and a something-that-notices and to take this to require the introduction of some individual or relation that my account does not recognize. This temptation might be reinforced by the fact that we began above by "looking within" and noticings are not obvious candidates for what is known by looking within. This fact is at best puzzling; at worst it might be thought that my inclusion of noticings under "sensations" is a mistake. In the present section we must address these temptations, puzzlements, and suspicions and show that they do not grow into solid objections.

Much of the difficulty about noticings will prove to be traceable to the fact that both "sensation" and "noticing" have uses that carry implications about the relations in which their referents stand. We may begin by sorting out some of these implications. To call something a sensation is often to imply that it is not caused by a physical object that has the same quality as the sensation. This is evident in the case of bodily sensations: the cause of a pain is not a pain, the cause of an itch is not an itch, and so on. Turning to afterimages, we know that the cause of a yellow oval afterimage is not yellow (it would be the complementary color, blue) and need not be oval (since it could be circular and not perpendicular to the line of sight of the afterimager). G# ringings in the ears are not caused by G# sounds; bitter aftertastes are as likely to be caused by something sweet as by something bitter; and so on. Causal connections, however, can never be essential to what a thing is. It is therefore possible to have a word that stands for the items to which "sensation" refers but that abstracts from any commitment to the nature of their causes. I have been using the term "sensation" itself in this somewhat regimented way. This is why I have been able to include noticings under "sensations". To clarify this, however, we must say a little more about noticings.

One salient feature of noticing is that what is noticed is actual. This can be brought out by an example. Suppose I claim to have noticed the yellowish cast of some marble. If you think it is perfectly white you will deny my claim and accuse me of having illusions or a jaundiced eye. You may allow that I thought I noticed a yellowish cast of the marble, but not that I really did notice it. This feature of noticing is presupposed by a second one, namely that in unproblematic cases, any quality that I notice causally contributes to my noticing it. For example, if I really do notice the yellowish cast of some marble, as opposed to guessing that it has a yellowish cast or arriving at such a belief by an inference, the marble must not only be somewhat yellow, but its being so must be involved in the cause of my noticing.

This last point explains why there is an apparent conflict in characterizing something as both a sensation and a noticing. For if we attend to the penumbra of causal connotations that these terms sometimes have, it can look as if noticed qualities have to be in material things, and efficacious, while qualities of sensations can be neither. The way to dispel the appearance of conflict is to abstract from causal considerations. When we do this, we find only similarities between the cases we call "noticing (qualities)" and the cases we call "(having) sensations". It is on the strength of these similarities that noticings have been included under "sensations". We can also understand why noticings do not naturally strike us as something we find upon "looking within". For where we notice the quality of something, there is some material thing having that quality and causing our noticing. However, once we focus on the noticing itself as the effect brought about by the material thing, we can see its similarity to what occurs in cases in which the causal background is different and in which we would speak of sensations.

It may be helpful to restate this view from the other end, so to speak. Let us take an example and begin with the causes of a sensation. Looking at a blue light and then at a dark wall will produce groups of neurons that are firing in a certain way and that will have among their effects a yellow afterimage. Looking at a canary will also cause neurons to fire. It is very likely that, under some circumstances, the groups of neurons that are caused to fire by the canary, and the manner of their firing, will be very similar to those that are caused by the retinal aftereffects of the illumination by blue light. In any case, under some circumstances, looking at a canary will cause an ephemeral individual that, like the afterimage, is yellow. Taken by themselves these things are very similar. They are, however, unlikely to occur by themselves. They will typically occur in complexes; and these complexes will occur in people who have the kind of internal organization that permits the habits and abilities required for believing. Now if we have a yellow sensation and we believe that it is being caused by our looking at a yellow canary, we will say that we are noticing the color of the canary. If we believe we have a yellow sensation and that it is caused by our having just been illuminated by a blue light, we will say that we are having an afterimage. We may, in unusual cases, have no settled view about our causal situation. In this case we may correctly say that we are having a yellow sensation. This will be correct whether or not it turns out that our content is being caused by something that is yellow.

A few remarks are needed to forestall some misunderstandings of this discussion of noticings. First, I have just said that *under some circumstances* looking at a canary will bring about a yellow sensation. The point of this caution was to allow for the fact that in perfectly ordinary cases of perception we do not have sensations. For example, looking at a canary in the most ordinary circumstances will not cause us to have a yellow sensation. We will have such a sensation only if we become attentive (in a certain way) because we are surprised to find a bird here or because we have been warned to pay special attention to the color of the bird or because someone has raised a skeptical question while we are watching the bird or from some other, similar cause. That routine perception does not involve sensations should be obvious from reflection on certain very familiar cases. For example, we can be presumed to see the curves in a road, provided we keep our car in its lane; but we hardly notice the character of each portion of the road's shoulder, lines, potholes, and so on. We do not notice the blackness of the print on the pages we read—until, of course, someone points that fact out to us. Again, people must see the coffee cups that they regularly succeed in picking up and drinking out of; but their minds are typically elsewhere when they are conversing over a cup of coffee. Of course, in any of these cases, one *can* have a sensation. Moreover, one cause of having a sensation is to think of a philosophical problem about perception or sensation while one is perceiving. Further, if one conjures up a memory of a perception in a philosophical moment, in order to exhibit to oneself what perceiving is really like, one will very likely produce an image of perceiving accompanied by a sensation. This is the source of whatever resistance philosophers may have to the idea that perception need not be accompanied by sensations.

It is natural and correct to say, as we did in the last paragraph, that we will have a sensation with a perception only if we become attentive in a certain way. We must be on guard, however, against being misled by an incorrect understanding of attention. We will be misled if we think of a sensation as something that is attended to. This way of thinking will, in fact, lead back to the relational structure proposed by Moore, which I have already criticized. That is, we may reproduce the pattern of

an awareness being aware of a sensation

with a (mis)analysis of attentiveness as

an act of attention attending to a sensation.[11]

Then we will have to face such embarrassing questions as whether one could have just the act of attending without the sensation, and whether one could have a sensation that was not attended to. To avoid these embarrassments we must realize that when we are noticing the color of a canary it is the canary that is being attended to and that noticing its yellow color is one way of attending to it; that is, it is one of the things whose occurrence justifies us in saying that we are attending to the canary. We can, and should, think of having a sensation as a particular state of attention or a particular way of being attentive.

11. In other terminology, this same misanalysis appears as the idea that acts of attention (or awareness) are directed upon *sense-data*. The rejection of this analysis thus emphasizes and confirms the difference between my account and sense-datum theories that I pointed out in the discussion of Anscombe's view in Chapter I.

CHAPTER VI

Ends in Themselves

We have considered people as beings who have sensations, who have thinkings, and who have two kinds of self-unity. We may now turn to a feature of ourselves that in a certain sense rests on these others, namely the fact that we are ethical subjects. We are possessors of rights and duties, we are appropriate candidates for praise and blame, and we are ends in ourselves and not mere instruments for others. This feature, as we shall see in the next paragraph, can give rise to an argument that we must be not altogether physical. The primary aim of the present chapter will be to respond to this argument. My way of responding, however, leads naturally to a further question about the connection between sentience and ethics. I shall take up this question in the last section of this chapter.

The argument that being an ethical subject requires a non-physical element is very familiar. Because of this and because we need only a preliminary formulation at this point, we can be quite brief. We may begin with the premise that being an ethical subject requires being *free*. But being purely physical, it is alleged, is incompatible with being free. Therefore, if human beings were purely physical, they could not be free and could not be ethical subjects. That being purely physical is incompatible with being free may be argued for in the following way. Every event that takes place in a purely physical thing is either caused by preceding events or is uncaused in the manner of the small-particle events that are described by quantum mechanics. Causation by a chain of events stretching as far back into the past as you like is incompatible with being free. Causation by a small-particle event that is itself uncaused is, however, also incompatible with being free. This is because being free requires being able to carry out concerted efforts over a period of time. These efforts must fit with one's perception of circumstances in such a way that, if the perceptions are correct, one's intentions are carried out. Such concerted efforts would, however, be impossible if one's actions were brought about by randomly occurring events. Now, if we were purely physical, our actions would be either the last members of causal series stretching back indefinitely or the last members of causal series originating in a quantum-mechanically indeterminate event. Since neither case is compatible with freedom, they would not be done freely.

In order to come to terms with this argument, we must develop our ideas of what an ethical subject is. To do this we must have some views about ethics and about metaethics. This fact forces the present chapter to have a somewhat tentative character. Evidently, I cannot insert here a book on metaethics; yet that is what it would take to establish fully all the premises that we will need in this chapter. The best I can do is, first, to be clear about what ethical assumptions will be required and, second, to choose premises that will be as widely accepted as possible. Strictly speaking, my conclusions can only be that *if* the premised ethical views are acceptable *then* certain results can be obtained. However, I believe that the metaethical view I shall outline is defensible and will be recognized by many as being so. Thus I believe that many readers will be able to detach my results and assert them non-hypothetically.

Metaethical Background

In what follows I shall sometimes refer to an "ethical system". An ethical system is, in part, a set of rules. The term "system" is used because the rules in the set composing an ethical system are interconnected, some rules, for example, telling how others are to be applied, how exceptions are to be made, or how excuses may be framed. It is essential not to fall into abstraction, however. We must keep in mind that what people believe to be ethical does sometimes have an effect on their behavior and that blame is not only sometimes deserved but is sometimes actually applied, to the consequent suffering of the person blamed. Thus, when we think of an ethical system, we must think of a system of rules that is actually used by people, sometimes to figure out what they should do and sometimes to justify the blame that they apply to others. We can remind ourselves of these observations with the following statement.

(ME1)   Ethical systems are systems of rules and practices
that apply to what the members of a community do.

Ethical systems concern actions at least in so far as they impinge or may impinge on others. Even if some action has never been contemplated some rule in an ethical system may apply to it. There seems to be no kind of action that might affect others but that lies outside potential coverage by a rule of an ethical system. Let us summarize these remarks with

(ME2)   In so far as an action may impinge on others it is a
proper object for application of an ethical system.

An ethical system is, of course, not the same thing as a legal system. A legal system is a system of laws and laws are enactments of a political body. Ethical rules may *also* be politically enacted; for example, the prohibition against murder is both a prohibition of our ethical system and a law. But it is not political enactment that makes a rule part of an ethical system. If argument for this is needed, this one is appropriate: Laws are supposed to be at least not unethical, that is, not in violation of ethical rules. This is not merely to say that laws are supposed to be consistent with each other (although this is also true). Therefore, the set of ethical rules cannot be identical with the set of laws. Further, one can offer ethical considerations for or against a law and one can do this without quoting any other laws.

Despite the differences between ethical and legal rules, there is one similarity. This is that violations of ethical rules as well as laws carry punishments. Punishments for violations of ethical rules that are not also laws are informally administered and not generally as severe as some legal penalties but they are real enough. To behave unethically is often to risk withdrawal of love by those who matter in one's life and withdrawal of trust, which may be necessary to carry on one's livelihood. It is to risk encountering difficulty in acquiring friends. If one has long accepted the ethical system that one has violated, one may also suffer guilt and self-loathing.

The punishments that attach to violations of ethical rules are essential to the continuance of an ethical system. We are all familiar with cases of ethics being given mere lip service and with wrongs that are overlooked. But if there were not *sometimes* undesirable results contingent upon unethical behavior (and praise contingent upon some cases of maintaining ethical behavior in the face of temptation) then our ethical injunctions would be truly empty. We should also recognize that "overlooked wrongs" are often merely actions that those who overlook them do not really believe to be wrong. People who *really* believe that something is wrong and are not themselves giving in to the same temptation usually do apply criticism and blame. The key point, however, is that the application of blame is essential to an ethical system's remaining a real part of people's lives. If there never were any consequences, there would cease to be observance and there would cease to be a point in teaching ethical rules. Let us record this point in

(ME3)   Ethical systems are maintained by actual application of blame for violation of their rules.

In making any use of an ethical system, even if one is only explaining the rightness of one's own actions, one is subscribing to that system and is thus implicitly threatening to apply the usual penalties for violation. To the extent that one does this, one supports the continuance of the system; that is, one enhances the probability that others will take its injunctions seriously in guiding their own behavior and that they will appeal to its rules to determine when blame is appropriate. This, in turn, exposes one to possible penalties for future violations. Now, even if one is not intending to do anything unethical in the future, it would be irrational to open oneself to potential penalties for something one *might* want to do in the future unless there were some perceived gain in so doing. We may thus conclude that

(ME4)   Those who use ethical systems usually believe that
          the existence of their ethical system is a good thing.[1]

It is obvious enough why people commonly believe that the existence of at least something like their ethical system is a good thing: they believe that if there were no such system, people would behave in ways that would have undesirable consequences for themselves.

If people did not commonly believe that the existence of their ethical system was a good thing, they would act in ways that would tend to undermine it. If such a lack of appreciation for an ethical system were sufficiently widespread, this tendency would be so strong that the system would no longer be maintained as a real part of people's lives. Stated contrapositively, this comes to

(ME5)   People's believing that the existence of their ethical
          system is a good thing is a causally necessary
          condition of the continuance of that system.

1. By "using an ethical system" I do not mean just thinking through what it says. I mean doing anything that might indicate to another person that one was allowing it to guide one's actions. This includes, of course, making explicit appeals to ethical principles in justifying one's actions to another person; but it might involve nothing more than acting like a person who says "Such and such a kind of behavior is good (or bad)." This would be sufficient to indicate subscription to an ethical system in any case where others would normally take an action to indicate belief that such and such a kind of behavior is good (or bad).

Reflection on (ME5) can make it tempting to say that ethical systems are *for* some benefit of their users. The origin of this temptation is that the situation here is analogous to some biological cases in which one says that an organ is *for* a certain purpose. For example, just as one says that lungs are *for* breathing, on the ground that it is their providing of respiratory function that causes them to continue to exist in descendants of animals that have lungs, so one might say that ethical systems are *for* their users' benefit on the ground that their producing some benefit is what causes them to be maintained as living societal rules-carried-out-into-practice. This way of putting things is not only tempting but actually legitimate and it provides a useful way of looking at ethical systems. I shall, nonetheless, usually avoid speaking in this way because I want to be absolutely sure that a certain confusion is not made. This is the confusion between

(i) Ethical systems are for their users' benefit,

for whose truth I have just argued, and

(ii) When people use an ethical system, they act in order to secure their own benefit.

(ii) is false if it is meant to hold in general. That is, there may be special occasions on which our ethical system either permits or enjoins people to act on their own behalf; but it is in the nature of ethical systems that in following their rules, people may be enjoined to do things for others' benefit, even at cost to themselves. Further, people need not and typically do not calculate the costs and benefits of acting ethically. For mature people of good character, the perception that their ethical system clearly requires something is ordinarily enough to lead to their decision without further ado.

There are, of course, unclear cases that lead to ethical perplexity. Some of these involve questions of application, that is, questions about what an ethical system actually requires in a particular case.

A more interesting kind of perplexity arises when it is suspected that some part of one's ethical system ought to be replaced by some other rule. One may come to think that it would be "more ethical" if people stopped living by one rule and started living by an alternative. For example, it has been a part of our ethical system that people must do all they can to preserve the life of another person (barring enemies in a battle and those being legally executed). But many have come to question whether this rule is really "right" in its unqualified form. They have wondered whether exceptions ought not to be made when the other person is very old and very sick, and when the means are very expensive and do not promise a return of a good quality of life.

The idea of giving an argument for this kind of change in ethical rules can be made to appear paradoxical. In arguing for such a change, we must argue for a change in what people do that affects others. Thus, we must argue about a matter that already comes under an ethical system. But since we are to give an ethical argument, we must presuppose our ethical system. Thus, it appears that we must use our ethical system to argue against itself. This paradoxical appearance is easily dispelled, however. We may begin with a point that is correct although still apparently problematic:

(ME6)   Arguments for ethical reform must aim to show that some revision of our ethical system would result in our having a better ethical system.

This is obvious enough, but we should dwell for a moment on its connection with (ME5). Arguments for ethical reform are arguments aimed at getting people to change their behavior. People will change their behavior (through persuasion) only if they can be shown that this is a good thing, and a better thing than not changing. They must be shown that the revised ethical scheme will be an improvement if they are to behave in such a way as to keep the revised ethical system in place as a living system.

What remains problematic about (ME6) is the fact that it has the term "better" in it and this is, of course, a term of ethical evaluation. This problem can be removed by the following Addendum to (ME6).

(ME6A)   "Better ethical system" in (ME6) means "ethical system that more effectively promotes all those things that are already considered good, apart from the behavior that is the subject of the proposed revision."

This formulation has the advantage of allowing ethical systems to depend on the material circumstances of their users without reducing ethics to management of material conditions. Thus, for example, suppose that some proposal is made whose main virtue is that it would tend to increase the amount of food available. If rights are already considered valuable, (ME6A) allows for their preservation to be offered as a relevant consideration in deciding whether to accept the proposal as a revision in our ethical system. It seems that, at present, appeals to the value of property rights convince most people that some kinds of interference with land use would be unethical. If, however, it were to appear likely that we will all starve to death unless severe conservation measures are practiced and that they will very probably not be practiced without government interference, it would be reasonable to expect that people's ethical views about property rights would change.

We should make explicit something that has been implicit for the last two paragraphs. Arguments for ethical reform aim to change the rules of an ethical system. They will not succeed unless they get people to follow the new rules, to teach them to their children, and to apply blame according to them. They will not ultimately succeed unless they persuade a large number of people to do these things. This will not happen unless a large number of people are persuaded that the revised system is better than the old one. So ethical arguments must aim at persuading a large number of people that the revised system is better than the old one. This fact gives the proposer of an ethical reform a motive to make the reform as appealing as possible to as large an audience as possible. This aim will be served very well if the proposed rule is perceived to be fair. Thus, each proposer of an ethical reform has a motive to cast the proposed rule in a way that will make it appear fair. People are not in general too stupid to perceive the effects of proposed ethical reforms. Thus, in general, the requirements of arguing for ethical reforms tend to make proposed reforms fair. Let us summarize these remarks as follows.

(ME7)   Arguments for ethical reform must appeal as widely as possible.

(ME8)   The requirements of arguments for ethical reform cause proposed ethical reforms to approximate to being fair.

The facts about what an ethical system is and what arguments for ethical reform require have implications about what abilities must be possessed by participants in groups that employ ethical systems. Such participants must be able to *do* something; otherwise, they would not be able to act on ethical rules, nor would any of their movements be fit objects of praise or blame. But they must also be rational, that is, at least rational enough to recognize when a rule applies and to calculate what an applicable rule enjoins. We can put these requirements shortly by saying

(ME9)   Participants in an ethical community must be rational agents.

(ME1)–(ME9) and their explanations leave very many questions quite open. This is an advantage for them, since people who disagree about the questions that are left open can accept (ME1)–

(ME9). Despite the fact that these statements leave so much open and, so to speak, indicate only the outlines of ethical reasoning, they are enough to give us a vantage point from which we may obtain some enlightenment on the questions to follow.

Free Will

We may now return to the argument that I stated briefly at the beginning of this chapter. This argument, as I remarked, is familiar. So are the main outlines of my response to the argument, which will be recognized as a variant of the view known as "compatibilism". Certain points in many formulations of compatibilism are either misstated or unstated and certain problems about compatibilism are often not squarely faced. I shall center my discussion on these points, where development and clarification are needed. We shall find that the metaethical view I have just introduced will not affect the early parts of our discussion but that it will become relevant at the end.

I shall begin by arguing for the following claim about the Causal Background of our Actions.

(CBA)   If we trace back through the series of causes leading up to our actions, we can always find an event over which we had no control.

I shall understand "the series of causes leading up to our actions" in such a way that it includes the action itself as the last (that is, latest) term of the series. This guarantees that there is such a series for every action, even if one were to hold that the action has no cause: this would just be a degenerate case in which the action is also the earliest member of the series. However, I do not expect anyone to find this degenerate case interesting. It is evident that the movements that constitute our actions are caused by muscle contractions and that these are caused by neural impulses.[2] Those who think there are earliest terms of some causal series leading up to our actions usually put them at some point earlier than the neural impulses that cause muscle contractions.[3]

The argument that I will state for (CBA) is a dilemma whose disjunctive premise is this: For each of our actions, the causal series leading up to it either (a) stretches back in time without end or (b) does not. Suppose that (a) holds of some action of mine, say, A_1. Then we can trace back through the series of its causes as far as we like. In particular we can find an event that is in the series and that occurred before I was born. I take it as an axiom that I had no control over any event that happened before I was born. Thus there is an event in the causal series leading up to A_1 over which I had no control. Since this point is generalizable for any action of any person, (CBA) is verified for case (a).

Let us turn to case (b). If the series leading up to one of my actions, say, A_2, does not stretch back in time without end, then there is at least one event, E in the series of which the following holds: there is no event that is both in the series and (wholly) earlier than

2. Not every action involves a movement. My *not* voting may, for example, be a very significant action, for which I may rightly be praised or blamed; but this action may involve sitting perfectly still. To avoid tediousness, I shall simply ignore such cases. They really are just like the cases that involve movement, for they are not cases of mere relaxation, but cases in which there is muscular contraction (tension) which, however, keeps one in place. The causal story and ethical conclusions about *that* kind of muscular activity are the same as for any other kind. These cases are, of course, different from omissions. For present purposes, omitting to do X can be treated as doing Y, where (a) Y is incompatible with X and (b) X is in some respect something one ought to have done. Y *may*, of course, be an action that involves no movement, for example, standing one's ground, refusing to save a drowning victim, remaining seated when the Queen enters the room (not out of ignorance but out of laziness), and so on; but Y *need not* be such an action.

3. See, e.g., J. C. Eccles, *Facing Reality* (New York: Springer-Verlag, 1970), chap. 8, esp. p. 119.

$E.$[4] (If for every event in the series there were another event that was in the series and earlier than it, the series would, as we shall see, stretch back in time without end.) E has no cause—for if it did, its cause would be an event that came earlier than it and is in the series. Now the concept of control is not a particularly clear one; but it is plain that it *somehow* involves causality. Thus we can be clear that if an event had no cause, it was not an event over which something had control; and thus it was not an event over which I had control. Thus E is an event over which I had no control. The point is generalizable for any action of any person. Thus, (CBA) is verified for case (*b*). But (*a*) and (*b*) are all the possible cases. Therefore (CBA) is verified for all cases.

The statement of the argument for case (*b*) may strike the reader as needlessly complex. It will, perhaps, forestall a misunderstanding if I explain why it has to be stated the way it is. To see the point, let us try a simpler statement, namely, that in case (*b*) there must be an earliest member of the series (which therefore has no cause and is thus not under my control). This might draw the objection that there being an earliest event in the series does not follow from the assumption of case (*b*). The reason is that the case (*b*) assumption can be satisfied by the following possibility. Let T be the moment of time that is located two minutes before A_2. Now suppose that there is a series S of causes leading up to A_2 such that for every element in S there is an earlier member and some member occurs sooner than any time after T that you care to name, but no member occurs either simultaneously with or earlier than T. Then there will not be an earliest member of the series S and, so it seems, there will not be any cause of A_2 that has no cause and is thus not under my control. This

4. E_1 is wholly earlier than E_2 just in case E_1 ends before E_2 begins. It will not be considered sufficient if E_1 begins before E_2 begins but is not over before E_2 begins. Unless the contrary is indicated, "earlier" means "wholly earlier". The reason for this usage is that it goes naturally with the principle that causes must precede their effects.

proposal is no doubt a little bizarre, but since I want (CBA) to be quite firmly established, I want to deal properly with this case.

Let us begin with an intuition about this proposal. My own first and persisting reaction to it is this: "So what if there is an infinite series of causes stretching back as close as you like to two minutes ago. If the whole series is just *there,* if it just springs up into existence, that's just as good (or as bad) as having a finite series beginning with an uncaused event. If I made the series come into existence, then, after all, there is a cause of the series that comes before it. But this is contrary to the assumption of the proposal. So, I didn't make the series come into existence. But if I didn't do that, what can it matter, as far as my control goes, what structure the series has?" Happily, this intuition can be given a more formal expression that firmly supports its appropriateness. To do this we must direct our attention to events that can be identified by the following formula:

event such that for all events, E, E is a part of the event just in case (i) E is in the series S and (ii) E occurs at or before $T + dt$.[5]

Let us specify dt as 10 seconds. The formula so specified identifies some event. Call it E_{10}. E_{10} is a cause of some events in the series S that occur after $T + 10$ seconds.[6] So E_{10} is a member of the series of causes leading up to A_2 (although it is not a member of the subseries S). Let us call this series S^*. There is not any member of S^* that is wholly earlier than E_{10}. (There are, of course, members of S^*

---

5. It is, of course, a key assumption that this formula really does identify an event. It would be a long story to explain why it does. Fortunately, this story has already been told in admirable detail in J. J. Thomson, *Acts and Other Events* (Ithaca, NY.: Cornell University Press, 1977). See esp. chap. 6. The statement of the operative principle here, the Principle of Event-Fusion, occurs at pp. 78–79.

6. *Ex hypothesi,* some event that is part of E_{10} causes some event that comes after $T + 10$ seconds. Call this later event E'. If E_{10} occurs, so does the part that causes E'. So, if E_{10} occurs, E' occurs; that is, E_{10} causes E'. See, again, Thomson, *Acts and Other Events,* pp. 65–66.

that end earlier than the end of E_{10}—for example, E_8, where E_8 is the event identified by the above formula when we set $dt = 8$ seconds.) E_{10} has no cause—for if it did, there would have to be an event in S^* that is earlier than it, that is, that occurs at or before T, contrary to the assumptions of the present case. So E_{10} meets the conditions asserted of "E" in my initial statement of the case (b) argument. We may not, however, call E_{10} the earliest member of the series, for there is an infinitude of events than which there is none earlier in the series—E_8, E_7, . . . $E_{.5}$, $E_{.003}$, and so on.

The force of this discussion will perhaps be clearer if we think of case (b) as dividing into two sub-cases. In (b_1) the series of causes leading up to my action stretches back some finite number of terms and then stops in an earliest term, which cannot, of course, have a cause. (For such a cause would be an earlier term in the series.) In case (b_2) there is a series of causes leading up to my action that stretches back an infinite number of terms, but all within a finite time (that is, the time stretches back as close as you like to, but not including, two minutes before the action). What we have lately seen is that in this case too, there is a cause of a cause . . . of a cause of my action, which has no cause and is thus not under my control.

I turn now to an objection to (CBA) and to my argument for it. This objection is that I have left out the possibility that some event in the series of causes leading up to an action is *self-caused*. Self-causation, the objection continues, opens up the possibility that some event in the series of causes leading up to an action is both (i) not caused by something earlier than it and yet (ii) under our control.

The proper reply to this objection is as brief as it is familiar. It cannot be the mere existence of the self that causes an event leading up to an action, because if it were, we would be doing that action all the time that we (the same self) existed. So we must think of being caused by myself as being caused by some event, E^* involving myself, for example, my coming to have a certain property, my coming to be in a certain state, or my undergoing a certain change. We can ask about the cause of this event. If we say that E^* is caused, we have taken the first step on the road that must end either in case (a) or in case (b). If we say that E^* is uncaused, then we are already at the place where the argument for case (b) can be offered. If we say that E^* in turn is self-caused, we merely postpone the agony. For we will now need an event, E^{**} that takes place in ourselves and brings about E^*; and one can reiterate the same set of alternatives for E^{**}.

These remarks run counter to a view articulated by Roderick Chisholm.[7] Let us therefore examine what he says to see if it reveals a mistake in our reasoning: "If a man does something that causes a certain event p to happen, then, *ipso facto,* he contributes causally to his doing something that causes that event p to happen. It is a mistake, therefore, to say that nothing causes his causing that event to happen" (71).[8] The key words in this passage are "*ipso facto*". If people cause the causings of their actions *by the very fact* that they cause their actions, then we will not have to look for *another* event in the self to explain how the causing of an action is caused by the self. If we can indeed avoid introducing such another event for this purpose, then we cannot arrive at (CBA). For we will be unable (at least by anything we have said) to rule out the claim that in causing its causing of an action to happen, a self is exercising control over whether or not it causes an action.

This certainly is an important result, if it can be established. But can it be established? From what does Chisholm derive it? The key

7. See Roderick Chisholm, *Person and Object* (London: G. Allen & Unwin, 1976), chap. 2. Parenthetical numbers in the following paragraphs refer to pages of this work.

8. The objection to which this passage is a reply tacitly assumes that if (CBA) is true, people will not be able to be held responsible for their actions. Whether this is so is a question to which we will shortly turn. It should be noted, however, that nothing has yet been assumed either way about this question, nor will our discussion of Chisholm require us to assume anything about it.

element in the derivation is definition D.II.10, the relevant part of which I will quote.

> D.II.10 *s* contributes causally at *t* to *p* = $_{DF}$ Either
> (a) . . . or (b) there is a *q* such that *s* undertakes *q* at *t* and s-undertaking-q is *p*, or (c) . . . . (70)

Since this is a disjunctive definition, the meeting of clause (*b*) is sufficient for the *definiendum* to hold. The relevance of this to the above-quoted conclusion is this. An undertaking is causally contributory to the action that was undertaken. So, if *s* does *q*, then *p*, that is, *s-undertaking-q*, causally contributes to *q*. Applying the definition, we have that *s* contributes causally to something he does (namely, undertaking *q*), which contributes causally to his action.

"Contribute causally" is not a new term, so it is clear that D.II.10 is not a stipulative definition. We are thus entitled to ask what reason Chisholm gives us for including (*b*) as sufficient for the correct application of the *definiendum*. The answer is as follows. Once again, I will cite only the relevant parts of the text.

> [L]et us now attempt to characterise a broader concept of agent causation that we may express by saying '*s* contributes causally to *p*'. We wish to construe this broader concept in such a way that we may say each of these things:
> (a) . . . .
> (b) If a person undertakes something, then he contributes causally to his undertaking that something.
> (c) . . . . (70)

Plainly, this will not do. Wishing to say something is not a justification for saying it. It does not show that there isn't an excellent reason for not saying it, namely, incoherence. Since we do not have a genuine argument at this point we do not have any reason to think that there must be something wrong with the case made for (CBA). We are not entitled to the "*ipso facto*" in the first passage quoted from Chisholm. We can still hold that people can causally contribute to some event that in turn causes their action. But we have seen no reason against supposing that such a contributing will have to be a distinct event from the one to which it causally contributes. We have seen no reason to add an alternative to the ones I have argued lead to (CBA). More strongly, we have not had such an alternative made intelligible to us.

Having, as I believe, established (CBA) let us turn to the question of its significance. The issue here concerns two Incompatibility Claims and a Connecting Principle.

(IC1)   (CBA) implies that people's actions are not under their control.

(CP)   In so far as people's actions are not under their control, they are not free and responsible agents.

(IC2)   (CBA) implies that people are not free and responsible agents.

Since I am sure both that people are sometimes free and responsible agents and that (CBA) is true, I am sure that (IC2) is false. However, I do not think there can be a conclusive argument against it. One of the things I shall do is to explain why this is so. Before doing that, however, I shall argue against a principle that I believe to be the key motivation for those who accept (IC1). I shall call this principle "the principle of Transitivity of Non-Control". It may be stated as follows.

(TNC)   If an event E is caused by an event over which C has no control, then E is an event over which C has no control.

(CBA) implies that for any action of C's, there is some event in its causal history over which C has no control. Take some effect of this event. (TNC) tells us that this effect is an event over which C has no control. Now reiterate this piece of reasoning. This will yield the result that the effect of this effect is an event over which C has no control. After enough reiterations, we will arrive at C's action, which (TNC) will, at the last, show to be an event over which C has no control. The point is generalizable for all actions of all people. Thus (TNC) leads to (IC1).

(TNC) is plausible because there are cases in which an event is both not under my control and caused by something not under my control, and in which the first of these facts seems dependent on the second. For example, my knocking your drink out of your hand might not be under my control because that event was caused by your dog's unexpectedly jumping up on me and knocking me off balance. Of course, if I had snapped my fingers in order to get your dog to jump up, its jumping would have been under my control and then my knocking your drink out of your hand might have been under my control—that is, it would have been under my control if I had known that that would be the result of the dog's jumping up. But if, as is implied by saying the jumping was unexpected, the dog's behavior was not under my control then it seems clear that my knocking your drink out of your hand was not under my control either.

There are, however, cases that are not so very much more complex, in which it is easy to see how (TNC) fails. Consider the thermostat in my living room. Consider also the event that is the first turning on of my furnace after the thermostat was installed. This event was under the control of the thermostat. Yet it was also the effect of causes over which the thermostat clearly had no control— the making of the thermostat, its being hooked up to the furnace, the whole system's current being turned on, and the temperature in the room at the time. I am, of course, not concluding from this that the thermostat is a free and responsible agent, but only that certain events are under its control despite the fact that there are events in their causal histories that are not under its control.

Let us have a second case. We may imagine a treasurer of the Stone Foundation who has a recipe for every decision about whether or not to sign for a disbursement from the foundation's funds. We may imagine that this officer is a stickler for form, and that he has learned his recipes for disbursing funds from certain books or from certain respected superiors who have in the past instilled in him a strong attachment to these recipes. We may further imagine that his acceptance has depended on authority relationships, so that if his superiors had suggested tighter or more lax recipes, our treasurer would have followed those. Now, we could hardly say of such a person that the disbursements from the foundation are not under his control. Yet whether or not they are made is due to events over which he had no control, because they were utterances of others who were his superiors or even words written by people who were dead before they had their effects on him.

It may be useful for the imagination to consider a variant of this case. Here, we are to suppose that specific recipes for decision have not been instilled. Instead, our treasurer has been indoctrinated with certain general principles and he has received a rigorous training in how these principles are to be applied. What lies behind particular disbursement decisions is somewhat more complex in this case than in the last one and making those decisions requires a little more effort on the part of the treasurer. But even if we suppose that the procedure for applying the general principles is quite rigid and predictable, we would not think we had depicted a man who is not in control of whether or not money is paid out.

What these examples suggest is that (TNC) breaks down when the series of effects of an event that is not under C's control includes the coming into existence of C, where C is the kind of thing that can be in control of some kind of event. If we call such a thing a "center of control" we can put this result very succinctly: the concept of a center of control that has been caused to come into existence and to begin operating is not a self-contradictory concept. That a center of control comes into existence and begins to work, that is, to exercise control, is not something that is under its control. It does not follow that the effects of the operation of such a center are not under its control, even though such effects result from the making of the center of control together with surrounding conditions that are also not under its control. The same result holds if we imagine uncaused centers of control, although this is very much harder to do. If thermostats were apt suddenly to appear on walls with their connections to furnaces in place and no one could find any regular antecedents for such occurrences—or even if we had a well-tested theory showing that there could be no regular antecedents—that would not lead us to abandon the idea that the ignitings of furnaces can be under the control of thermostats.

We must be clear that I am holding only that there *can* be events that are under the control of a center of control which is itself brought about by events that are not under its control. I am *not* holding that being caused by a center of control is *sufficient* for an event's being under that center's control. We have already seen a case in point. I am (among other things) a center of control and I may cause your drink to leave your hand; but if this happens because I have been knocked into you by your dog, that event is not under my control. Analogously, we may imagine a furnace starting because I take one contact in the thermostat and wire it to the other. The thermostat in this case is involved in the causal chain leading to the igniting of the furnace but no one will say that it is a bad instrument if the room gets warm. One could say in such cases that although a center of control is causally involved, it is so in a way that bypasses its characteristic operation.

The foregoing discussion may appear to depend heavily on certain facts about the usage of the word "control". This would be an objection if it could be sustained, because in that case I would have made only a verbal point. Such a point could at most force a reformulation of (CBA), (TNC), and (IC1) without cutting against the idea behind them. However, while the facts about the usage of "control" have proved convenient, they are not essential to my argument. They are what they are because of the following facts, which clearly do not depend on language. Ordinary tools, like hammers and screwdrivers, have no operations of their own, nothing that they themselves do. The details of their effects depend on details of the causes of their motion. For example, the place where the hammer strikes depends on where exactly my muscles have forced it to go. A little more pressure to the left will result in a proportional leftward hit and a little twist of the hand will result in a proportional obliqueness of the blow. Centers of control, however, do something that is properly attributed to their own operation. Because of their internal design, their outputs are not proportional to such things as the speed of their manufacture or the firmness with which they are screwed together. (There are, of course, limits that cannot be overstepped. If a thermostat is screwed together so tightly as to break its parts, or has its bulb completely full of mercury, it will not work. But there is a range within which variance in these and other respects does not matter.) Nor are their outputs proportional to the precise conditions of their use. For example, the operation of my thermostat does not depend on how fast I move the temperature lever in setting it. When the manufacture, installation, and setting of a thermostat are completed, there is something left for it to do. This doing is dependent on its internal structure and therefore is appropriately regarded as its own doing.

It may be thought that (TNC) can be argued for by considering the parts of centers of control. We can take these as small as we like, as small as, say, atoms. These are not centers of control. Neither their existence nor their coming together is under the control of the center of control that they compose; for that center cannot be in control of its own creation. Further, the motion of each atom is either uncaused, and thus not under the control of anything, or it is caused. If, however, it is caused, its causal lineage goes back either to an uncaused event (not under anything's control) or else to a time before the center of control came into existence. Thus, the argument continues, the motions of its atomic parts cannot be under the center's control. Everything that a center of control does, however, involves a motion of something composed of its (atomic) parts. Therefore, nothing that a center of control does is *really* under its control; there cannot be anything that really deserves to be called a "center of control".

This argument attempts to support (TNC) by appealing, in effect, to an analogous principle. We might call this analogue the principle of Transitivity of Non-Control via the Part-Whole relation and we can state it as follows.

(TNCPW)   Suppose some portion P of C is composed of parts $p_1, p_2, \ldots p_n$. Suppose M is a motion of P. Then, if the motions of $p_1 \ldots p_n$ are not under C's control, M is not under C's control.

This principle, so to speak, passes non-control from motions of parts to motions of wholes composed of those parts, whereas (TNC) passes non-control from causes to effects. We shall see, however, that it is a dubious principle. We must begin by removing an ambiguity. There is, of course, *a sense* in which control over the motions of parts of P *follows* from control over M. This is the sense in which I can be said to have moved the iron atoms in my arm in virtue of the fact that I moved my arm and those atoms were in my arm. In *this* sense it must of course be true that if M is under my control, the motions of the parts of P must also be under my control. The argument of the preceding paragraph. however, does not show that centers of control must lack control over the motions of the atoms that compose them in this sense. It moves from lack of what might be called independent control of atoms—that is, lack of ability to control the motions of single atoms independently of the motions of other atoms—to lack of ability to control motions of what is composed of them. Now, to claim that this move is logically valid would be to commit a fallacy of composition. It would be to sanction the form: Each part lacks the property F (in this case, the property of being under the control of C); therefore, the whole composed of those parts lacks the property F. Further, once the ambiguity of (TNCPW) has been removed, it is clear that it is false. Moving my arm is one example; such movement is under my control (usually) but I have no independent control of the atoms in my arm. Thermostats are further examples; they control furnace ignitings, but they do not have independent control over their atoms.[9]

(TNC) has a superficial plausibility because there are many cases that fit the pattern it suggests. If causal lines do not lead through a center of control then it seems that non-control is indeed passed on. For example, if the motion of one billiard ball is due to an earthquake, that is, is not under the control of a center of control, then the motions of balls that it hits are not under the control of such a center either. Also, as we have seen, even centers of control can be involved in causal transactions that bypass their control. None of this, however, supports (TNC) as a general principle. We have articulated the kind of case that constitutes an exception to it and have turned aside attempts to rescue it.

9. The point here is related to one made by Hilary Putnam in "Reductionism and the Nature of Psychology", *Cognition* 2 (1973): 131–146. The explanation of why a square peg does not fit into a round hole lies in its shape, not in some story about the interaction of electrons in the peg with electrons in the rim of the hole. Yet the latter cause the non-passage of the peg and the motion (or lack of it) of the peg is in some sense nothing other than the motion of the electrons and other particles that compose it. To put the point in the direction parallel to the analogy here, we can say that even though none of the (small) parts are the explanation, it does not follow that the whole composed of them has no properties that are the explanatory ones. Likewise, a center of control controls, even though it does so by moving parts that are composed of parts that are neither centers of control nor items over whose minute motions the center has independent control.

In showing that (TNC) is false we have not strictly proved that (IC1) is false; but we have removed the main reason for affirming it. In doing this, we have also removed one reason for believing (IC2), namely, the reason that arrives at (IC2) via (IC1) and (CP). This reason is sufficiently important that removing it ought to cause one to have serious doubts about (IC2). However, I have said that a conclusive argument against (IC2) is not possible. It is time to explain why this is so.

To *establish* the falsehood of (IC2) one would have to be able to *establish* that people are (sometimes) free and responsible agents. This has proved difficult to do. I shall propose an explanation for this difficulty. That this explanation is correct is again something for which I cannot offer a conclusive argument. I believe that by the end of our discussion, however, its correctness will have been made extremely plausible. The Explanation of the difficulties surrounding Free and Responsible agents is, briefly, this.

(EFR)   Whether something is a free and responsible agent is an ethical question; that is, it is a question that it is proper for the members of an ethical community to debate, where the character of the debate is roughly indicated by (ME3)–(ME7).

This explanation receives immediate support from the following points. Whether people deserve punishment or praise is a question that affects how they will be treated and is evidently an ethical question. Deciding this question depends, among other things, on deciding to what extent people are free and responsible agents. It is thus extremely plausible that this latter question is itself an ethical question. If this is correct, then to establish that people are sometimes free and responsible agents, one would have to establish that the outcome of fully considered ethical debate would result in people being considered to be (sometimes) free and responsible agents. It is extremely plausible that this is indeed the case, but one could hardly *establish* this result without going through a very long argument about what would be the best way to treat people.

(EFR) is further supported by the way in which people in fact debate questions of freedom and responsibility. It is true that arguments like the one involving (IC1) and (CP) come up in such discussions. People do not, however, proceed as if that were the only relevant kind of argument. If special treatment is proposed in some case, on the ground that someone is insane or the victim of circumstance, people do ask what would happen if we treated all who are similarly situated in the proposed way. The classification of people as free and responsible agents runs parallel to the decision whether or not it would be a good thing to regard all those like them as eligible for punishment (for bad actions) or praise (for good ones).

The fact that questions of control come up at all in the context of questions about free and responsible agents needs accounting for. This is because control looks like a factual matter that could not be a proper subject of ethical debate. The explanation is as follows. If we consider especially (ME3), (ME5), and (ME7) we can see that in a stable ethical system, there must be a normal presumption about its members, namely that they are eligible for the consequences that the rules of the system prescribe for various actions. Allowing exceptions, however, may result in a better ethical system; thus, in view of (ME6), the outcome of ethical discussion may be that some exceptions from prescribed consequences are made. (ME7) and (ME8), however, tend against making exceptions. A way of accommodating them to some extent is to make exceptions only for classes of cases, where one can argue that one's ethical system is improved by making an exception for the whole class. Now, to make such an argument, one must identify the class for which one means to make an exception. One cannot describe it only as the class of cases where it would be good to make an exception, because this does not provide others with a way of telling what class this is. So there is a need to describe a class of exceptions in a way that will be clear and that will not raise further ethical questions.[10] "Cases in which agents are not in control of their actions" is apparently a description of this type. So are, for example, "cases in which agents do not have the power to do otherwise" and "cases in which agents do not have the power to want to do otherwise".

There is, however, a difficulty with these descriptions. There are, to be sure, clear cases in which they apply and clear cases in which they do not apply. But there are also cases in which it is *not* clear whether or not they apply. It would be convenient if there were a purely factual way of resolving what ought to be done in such cases. In fact, however, their resolution is ultimately an ethical matter; that is, it is ultimately a question of what way of treating certain borderline cases would make for the best ethical system. The result of this situation is that in central cases, being in control, having power, and so on are pure matters of fact, but in borderline cases what ought to be counted as being in control and so on—that is, what we ought to treat as being in control and so on for the purposes of making or not making exceptions—is a proper matter for ethical debate and cannot be settled factually first, as a way of resolving ethical issues in a simple way.

These remarks should serve to explain how the idea of being a center of control can be a factual matter (in clear cases) and yet be connected to the idea of a free and responsible agent, even though this latter notion is an ethical one. They also, however, contain the explanation of why so many versions of compatibilism (of causation of actions and free and responsible agency) fail. The versions I have in mind are those that offer a sufficient condition of being a free and responsible agent—for example, "People are free and responsible

---

10. One could put the point this way: Fairness requires description of classes of exceptions in factual terms. Fairness is built into ethical systems by their very nature. Thus, the need for a fact/value distinction grows out of the nature of ethical systems themselves.

agents if they are in control of their actions" or ". . . if they could have done otherwise if they had wanted to" or ". . . if it was in their power to do otherwise." Each of these is plausible because (i) there are some clear cases where they apply and in which those to whom they apply are paradigms of people who should receive punishment or praise, depending on what they do, and (ii) there are some clear cases where they do not apply and in which those to whom they do not apply are paradigms of people who should be treated exceptionally. They fail, however, because they promise a purely factual resolution of who should be treated in what ways when in fact, *ultimately* the resolution of hard cases requires us to consider what would be the best ethical system. Since this is always the logical position, it should really not be surprising that opponents of such views can produce counterexamples to them.

Let us stop to summarize the results we have developed in this section. It seemed, let us recall, that the fact that we are ethical subjects might give us reason to believe that we cannot be wholly physical beings. From our present perspective we can say, first, that the problem about being free and responsible agents arises, not from our being physical, but from the fact that the series of events leading up to our actions is either thoroughly causal or has some uncaused event in it. This dichotomy holds whether the series of events leading to our actions is imagined to involve only physical things or whether it is supposed that it includes events of a non-physical kind. Physicality or non-physicality is thus not relevant to (CBA) and so (CBA) gives us no reason to think we are not wholly physical. We can say, second, that there is reason to doubt the truth of (IC2). We have not only removed its principal support but have explained how the existence of free and responsible agents is compatible with (CBA). We have, finally, seen why some attempts to explain this compatibility fail and we have understood why their failure does not undercut the view they seek to establish.

These are conclusions that we will not find reason to modify. There is, however, a problem that might seem to threaten the position at which we have arrived. This is the problem of who (or what) is to count as an ethical subject. In the following section I shall explain and resolve this problem.

Sentience and Ethics

(ME9) tells us that it is a necessary condition of being a participant in an ethical community that one be a rational agent. We can introduce the discussion to follow by raising the question whether this is also a sufficient condition. There are two things that suggest that it is. First, (ME1)–(ME8) do not seem to require anything further of ethical subjects, yet they describe principles whose following would make a community a community of ethical subjects. Second, and more positively, being a rational agent seems to be all that is required for being an ethical subject according to any form of contractualism. The idea that ethical systems either arise from or are justified by the willing agreement of their participants requires only (a) that these participants can do things that affect the well-being of other participants, (b) that the system be mutually beneficial, and (c) that the participant be capable of understanding and following the prescriptions of the system. But these conditions can be met by supposing that the participants are rational agents.

The question whether being a rational agent is sufficient for being an ethical subject will perhaps seem more interesting if we point out the main reason for answering in the negative: If this condition *were* sufficient, then there could be robots that were ethical subjects. Since this claim may seem surprising, however, and since it is necessary to see that it is true in order to proceed with the next step of the argument, I shall spend some time explaining and defending it.

Ethical Robots?

Let us first stipulate that a robot is non-sentient. This does not follow from its being artificial since, after all, we might learn how to manufacture a collection of organic molecules that would be indistinguishable from a "naturally produced" human being. In such a case the same causes of sensations and other contents would be present as would exist in a human being, and so such a being would be sentient even though artificial. But it would not be a robot as I intend the term.

It may be thought that we can rule out robots as ethical subjects on the ground that they cannot really be agents. This in turn might be thought to be the case because they don't *do* anything: they are just fancy instruments of those who manufacture and program them. We have already seen that the fact that robots are *made* does not show that they are not centers of control. Still, it might be thought that being a center of control is not rich enough for being an agent; after all, a thermostat is one kind of center of control, but clearly not an agent. Or it might be thought that the fact that a robot is *programmed* would be a particular kind of making that would preclude its being either a center of control or an agent. Both of these points can be answered if we can establish that robots could meet the following Conditions for Agency.

(CA1) There is a "personality" that pertains to the robot itself and not merely to the instructions it has at the moment.

(CA2) This "personality" is connected to some benefit for the robot.

(CA3) The way in which this "personality" is exercised in benefiting the robot is responsive to changing circumstances.

Each of these conditions requires some discussion.

The best-known example of a robot "personality" is Isaac Asimov's three laws of robotics.[11] These laws obviously have an ethical flavor but that is not the relevant point here. The reason why Asimov's laws form the "personality" *of the robot* is that they are permanent possessions of the robot. The robot cannot be got to violate them by being given any set of instructions. One would have to melt it down and make a different robot to get a robot whose "personality" did not embody the three laws. Robots with a "personality" are, of course, quite visionary from an economic point of view. People who pay for robots (or computers) want them to carry out instructions without interference from a "personality". But it would be *possible* to bestow on a robot some feature of operation that could be changed only by hardware restructuring and not by any set of instructions (or programming) presented to its input receptors.

A hard-wired feature of a robot's operation might be just a quirk if it were not connected to some benefit for the robot. For example, no one would credit a robot with an action—for example, lying or joking—if, whenever it gave a numerical output, the value was three more than the correct number. If we are to regard some movement of a robot as some action that it performs, we must be able to see the movement as providing some benefit for the robot, that is, as being a means to some end that the robot has. This observation may occasion an objection to the effect that there cannot really be a benefit *for a robot,* as opposed to its owner or user. As we shall see, there is

11. See Isaac Asimov, *I, Robot* (Garden City, N.Y.: Doubleday, 1950). The three laws are: (1) A robot may not injure a human being, or, through inaction, allow a human being to come to harm. (2) A robot must obey the orders given it by human beings except where such orders would conflict with the First Law. (3) A robot must protect its own existence as long as such protection does not conflict with the First or Second Law.

For a philosophical discussion of some issues relating to what I have called "personality", see Paul Ziff, "The Feelings of Robots", in A. R. Anderson, ed., *Minds and Machines* (Englewood Cliffs, N.J.: Prentice-Hall, 1964), pp. 98–103, and Ninian Smart's reply, "Robots Incorporated", in the same volume, pp. 106–108.

something to this objection; but it will not do as it stands. Cows are raised to be eaten and an illness in a cow is bad for the farmer who sought to profit from the cow and, less directly, bad for those who would have consumed it. There is, nonetheless, a clear sense in which an illness is bad *for a cow.* Analogously, there is a clear sense in which some things are bad for a robot, as well as for its users. If a robot is made of metal, for example, it will probably be bad for it if it gets wet. We can imagine many kinds of robots for which it would be bad if they got too hot. If these things are bad for robots then not getting wet and not getting too hot will be good for them. Under certain circumstances, so will getting sheltered, getting shaded, getting cooled, and so on. If a robot moved in such a way as not to get wet or in a way that resulted in its getting cooler when it was approaching a temperature that was too hot for it, it would be moving in a way that was good for it.

If all that a robot could do were to switch itself off (and thereby stop generating internal heat) whenever its internal temperature approached the danger point, *it* would not act even though it would meet (CA1) and (CA2). Contrast with this a robot that, within wide limits, does whatever is necessary to control its temperature.[12] We may imagine that it sometimes moves out of the sun but that at other times it closes venetian blinds. (For example, when closing blinds would require less energy expenditure than moving into shade or when blind closing would be more compatible with performing a task it has been instructed to carry out.) We may further imagine that after we inform it of the properties of alcohol, and when it cannot close blinds or move into shade, it spreads alcohol over its plates and holds out its arms to promote evaporation. Let us further imagine that it is persistent about these temperature control efforts and that, while we may be able to get it to adopt alternative strat-

12. The qualification "within wide limits" is essential. If we dropped it we would have to suppose our robot to be omniscient.

egies, there is nothing we can do by way of instruction (as opposed to taking it apart and refabricating it) that will result in its giving up all operations that tend toward keeping its temperature under a certain threshold. Here we have a picture of a being acting in a way that takes account of its own goals. It will be clear when it has acted successfully and when its action has been only incompletely carried out. The movements of such a robot will have the kind of directedness that will provide clear sense to remarks about what it is trying to do, even if it is unsuccessful. If we hide the alcohol on a hot day and see the robot opening cupboard doors, scanning, and then closing them, we will have adequate basis for saying it is looking for the alcohol. It will make good sense to say that the robot is acting as if it had just said, "I'm getting too hot." These facts support the conclusion that a robot of the kind we have imagined would correctly be said to act on its own behalf and therefore be an agent.

Our recent imaginings required us to suppose that a robot could, within wide limits, adjust its behavior so as to be responsive to changes in its environment. This requirement may lead to a series of objections, all having the form that we must credit to robots something that they cannot have. Thus one might say that robots could not have the flexibility to adjust their behavior to changing circumstances in the way envisaged. Or one might allow robots some degree of flexibility but not enough to be rational. Or one might say that a robot could be rational but not rational *enough* to be an ethical subject. This might be argued for on the basis of two further claims. First, one might hold that an ethical subject must be able not only to follow rules but to propose revisions and to evaluate arguments for reform. Second, one might suppose that robots could be rational enough to follow rules but not rational enough to engage in ethical reflection about them.

I know of no way to prove that a robot could be made that would be highly flexible or rational or rational enough to reflect on ethical rules. My response to the objections just stated will therefore be only negative. That is, I shall argue only that we do *not know* that there could *not* be a flexible, rational, and reflective robot. I shall do this, in turn, by explaining why apparent obstacles to there being such robots are not genuine obstacles, or are not known to be so.

The fact that a robot is physical should not be taken to be a bar to its having flexibility, rationality, or the ability to reflect on ethical rules. For none of these things involves having sensations. They do involve intentionality and the external unity described in Chapter V. These, however, have been given an analysis that did not require bringing in anything that is non-physical.

The fact that something is programmed is not *per se* a bar to its being flexible. Machines can be programmed to play chess. The authors of chess programs have not envisaged each possible chess position and given the machine a corresponding instruction. Because of this, every newly encountered position to which a chess-playing machine generates a reasonable response can be counted as a case in which some degree of flexibility has been exhibited. That chess is only a game is not relevant. On the one hand, the same point could be made about programs for medical diagnosis. On the other hand, one might regard temperature regulation as a "game" in which exceeding the threshold is "losing" and in which the "pieces" are sun, shade, blinds, hot air registers, alcohol, and so on. It is not evident that this "game" need be more complex than chess. Successful responses or even nearly successful ones to new circumstances would be clear instances of flexibility.

The most powerful argument that I know of, and that is directed against the possibility of a high degree of flexibility in a robot, is one that has been put forward by Hubert Dreyfus.[13] Dreyfus' own statements of this argument are intertwined with exhibitions of exaggerated claims made by optimists about artificial intelligence and ex-

---

13. See his *What Computers Can't Do: The Limits of Artificial Intelligence* (rev. ed.; New York: Harper & Row, 1979).

planations of difficulties that workers in that field have encountered. We may, however, state the core of the argument in a fairly simple and at least initially plausible way.

(D1)   Programs that can be received by machines must be written in the form of very explicit rules.

(D2)   Explicit rules must be stated in terms of some definite set of concepts.

(D3)   Flexibility of response (or intelligence, or rationality) requires the grasping of relevance (for example, the relevance of new elements in the environment).

(D4)   Relevance may be of indefinitely many kinds; that is, the respect in which one thing is relevant to another may be of one of an indefinitely large number of kinds. Therefore,

(D5)   Relevance may require an indefinitely large number of concepts for its expression. Therefore,

(D6)   The rules by which a machine is programmed cannot contain enough concepts to permit the recognition of much relevance. (Cf. (D5) and (D2).) Therefore,

(D7)   The capacity for flexibility (intelligence, rationality) cannot be programmed into a machine.

The point that I have tried to capture in this argument is extremely plausible in cases of the following sort. Suppose we set a machine to designing tools for use on small boats. We provide data on the shape of the human hand, its strength, a description of the task to be done, the properties of various materials, and, of course, formulas for calculating the stress that a tool will undergo if it is of this or that shape. Now, even if this machine has been given the physical properties of water and formulas for calculating relative specific gravities, it is unlikely to come up with an optimal solution. This is because whether a tool floats or not is a relevant feature when it is designed for a task to be done on a (small) boat. But unless we explicitly program the machine to take this into account, we cannot expect it to appreciate the relevance of whether the tool floats, and hence whether it should be made out of a light material rather than a heavy one.

However, while this is a persuasive case, I do not find it conclusive. We may begin to see why by getting clear that even people do not always appreciate relevance. They usually do not discover for themselves that the relevant feature of the letters in the series OTTFFSSENT . . . is that they are the initial letters of the names of the positive numbers, in order. They usually do not appreciate the relevance of facts mentioned by the authors of mystery stories until the detective with the superior grey cells reveals it to them. So if we ask whether robots could be flexible or rational we must not imagine that we are asking whether they could be *perfectly* rational or whether they could be *infallible* recognizers of relevance. A robot capable of the ratiocination required by (ME1)–(ME8) need only be able to respond to new circumstances in a way that has a reasonable chance of success, over a range of cases that approximates human abilities.

Existing programs, like chess programs and medical diagnostic programs, have *some* ability to recognize relevance. If, for example, a machine makes a good move at chess in a previously unencountered case, we could describe it as, say, having appreciated the relevance of the fact that the bishop is hemmed in. This could be a reasonable description even though its programmer never thought in terms of having it look for whether the bishop is hemmed in and even if the concept of being hemmed in was never in the programmer's mind at any stage of the formulation of the program. Since some ability to recognize relevance is available to machines, defenders of Dreyfus' conclusion need an argument that this ability cannot be extended to the degree that would allow us to say that, for example, within wide limits, a robot will do whatever is appropriate to control its temperature. Dreyfus does in fact have an argument of this kind. It is that relevance extends into all corners of our lives, so that we cannot really isolate any area from any other. For example, our behavior toward many people is mainly fixed by their jobs. In the case of talking to a salesperson, for example, the usually relevant concerns I would have are: Is what I want available? How much does it cost? What competing products are available? Is there a warranty? Asking and responding to such questions would form most of our conversation. But if the salesperson becomes sick or is engaged in a crime, or if it comes out by accident that we have a mutual friend, or a mutual interest, or come from the same place, then the appropriate contents of our conversation may relate to any number of things besides the product and its price.

This argument shows that relevance and flexibility of response within ordinary human limits is extremely complex. It does not, however, show that it is infinitely complex. It certainly suggests that a robot that could, within wide limits, do what was required to control its temperature would have to have a very long program and would have to have data on a very large number of items. But it does not show that the complexities would have to run on *forever,* that is, that there *could not* be a program that was long enough and a data base that was rich enough to permit the envisaged flexibility. There is one further point we should make in support of this (limited) conclusion. We need not suppose that what we would have to provide for a relevance-recognizing machine is something about each particular case of what might be a relevant feature. In our example about designing tools for boats better robotic performance might not have required that we tell it explicitly about the advantage of floating. A design for a floating tool might have resulted if the robot had been programmed with some of the physical properties of people and some economic principles along these lines: Tools have value; people do not like to be permanently separated from things they possess that have value. No doubt it is a formidable task to figure out how to get a machine to apply such principles. All rules, however, have some degree of generality. Thus, generality cannot *per se* be an obstacle to being programmable. The advantage of generality is, of course, that it enables many things at one stroke to become connected and potentially recognized as relevant.

Two brief additional points will reinforce doubts about Dreyfus' conclusion. First, although computers must be given definite rules, as (D1) says, it does not follow that rules must be stated in terms of concepts. We could, for example, give a mathematical description of the operation of some part of our body and then write a program for calculating according to that description. A machine that ran such a program would yield descriptions of bodily motions that would not (yet) be categorized as leaving, arriving, exercising, killing time, or as any of the things that a particular motion might turn out to be. Second, recently developed parallel distributed processing theories hold the promise of a solution to the relevance problem that is quite different in its inspiration from that of traditional approaches. Thus, even if Dreyfus' critique of existing strategies for relevance-recognition proves to be sound, there may still be a way of designing relevance-recognizing robots.[14]

I want to re-emphasize the weakness of the conclusion that I draw from all this and that I will assume in what follows. I do *not* conclude that we *will* be able to program a robot to exhibit a high degree of flexibility or rationality or the ability to reflect on ethics. I say only that we do not have a good reason to think that this is impossible. We have some idea of the abilities required for rationality and we have seen that these are present in some degree in existing machines. We are not entitled to suppose that it is a *simple*

14. See David Rumelhart, James McClelland, *et al.*, *Parallel Distributed Processing: Explorations in the Microstructure of Cognition*, vol. 1 (Cambridge, Mass.: MIT Press, 1986), esp. pp. 35–36 and 38–40.

matter to extend these abilities so as to achieve higher degrees of flexible response, nor that we already know how such extensions are to be made. But we have no defensible principle that shows that such higher degrees of flexibility are impossible for a robot to have. Nor can we argue that while a robot might be rational it could never be rational enough to reflect on ethical rules. The reason is that reflection on ethical rules does not seem to require anything specifically different from the abilities associated with rationality in general. It may require more in the way of flexibility of response or data than some other exercises of rationality but there is no argument that it must require more than could be given to a robot.

Conclusion

The conclusion of the last paragraph, weak though it is, permits us to claim that we are capable of *imagining* a robot that is rational and can reflect on ethical rules. We are aware of no contradiction in such an idea, and non-contradiction is a sufficient condition of imaginability in a wide sense of this term. There is, further, no difficulty in giving pictorial detail to such an imagined robot. Our science fiction has made it easy for us to spin our own tales of robots pointing out to us the unfairness of our procedures and refusing to cooperate in carrying out unethical commands.

Reflection on this imaginative possibility leads in the following direction. What we know we can imagine is that there could be a robot that could have all the abilities required for entering into a social contract.[15] If entering such a contract is sufficient for being an ethical subject, then we can imagine how a robot could be an ethical subject. But it seems that we really cannot imagine such a thing. To do so, we would have to imagine robots as having rights and duties, as being blameworthy for immoral actions, commenda-

15. See above, page 206.

ble for doing their duty, and praiseworthy for good works. This seems to be a strange and difficult, not to say ridiculous, task. We are thus led to the following problem. The difficulty in imagining a robot as an ethical subject is, we have seen, not due to failure to be able to imagine its entering into a social contract. But our meta-ethical account is a species of contractualism. So it may appear that something has been left out of our account, that there is something essential to ethics that is not captured in contractualism. If this is so, then our results earlier in this chapter, which depend on the assumption that (ME1)–(ME9) describe the essential features of an ethical system, are threatened. What I must do in the remainder of this section is to show how we can resolve the problem I have described without having to abandon either our earlier results or a contractualist approach to ethics. The first point we must make will, however, only make the problem sharper.

The obvious and correct reason why it is difficult to imagine a robot as an ethical subject is that it suffers no pains and enjoys no pleasures. This is the reason that I alluded to above that makes it seem plausible that there could not really be a *benefit* for a robot. What is actually true is that there are *some* benefits—avoidance of pain and provision of pleasure—that a robot cannot have. Yet even though there are other benefits, which we have seen a robot can have, the lack of *these* benefits *seems* to make a robot ineligible as an ethical subject.

The solution to the problem I have raised for the view I have taken (and for contractualism in general) is this. Robots are not, as far as we can show, incapable of being participants in a system that would have a structure that we would recognize as that of an ethical system. When we find the task of imagining them to be ethical subjects strange and difficult, we are really trying to imagine something different, namely, that they might be not only members of *some* ethical community but members of *our* ethical community. The barrier to imagining this is that to treat a robot as a participant in our ethical system would involve recognizing its right to secure benefits to itself even in cases where its doing so would cost one of us people some pain, or the foregoing of some pleasure. But avoidance of pain and pursuit of pleasure are too important to us for us to enter into a system that allows frustration of them for the sake of something not involving them. We are reluctant enough to agree to have our avoiding pain and pursuing pleasure frustrated by other people. Here, however, we at least have a compelling argument that everyone can see that they are just like us. So we have to put up with allowing others the right to secure benefits to themselves even when this means competition for us, because we can see that we have to agree to this in order to live with other people at all. A rational robot might have to agree to recognize the rights of other robots, in order to live under a system that in general would be very advantageous to it. *We*, however, have no such reason for allowing rights to *them*. We are in no danger of weakening the regard that other people have for our interests by taking this position. In denying robot rights, we are not denying the importance of respecting the purpose of avoiding pain and securing pleasure; for robots do not have pains or pleasures.

The consequences of this resolution are these. First, while we need to suppose that avoidance of pains and pursuit of pleasures is a very important purpose that people share, we do not need to suppose that the disvalue of pain and the value of pleasure are grounded in anything distinct from people's preferences. We thus do not need any account involving something non-physical to explain how we know about these values. Nor do we require any addition to the metaethical background given in the first section of this chapter. Being a participant in an ethical system does not by itself require anything non-physical. Being a participant in *our* ethical system does require something non-physical. The non-physical enters into our ethical system, however, only in the following way: To be a participant in our system, one must have among one's purposes the avoidance of pains or the pursuit of pleasures; to have such purposes, one must be capable of suffering pains or enjoying pleasures; to be thus capable is to be able to have sensations and other contents that we have seen in previous chapters to be non-physical.

This conclusion brings us back to a point made at the end of Chapter I. We saw there how it is possible for sensations to figure in our intentions without being causes of neural firings. We saw, that is, how we *can* have what we now see we need to have for the resolution of the problem I raised regarding ethics. This conclusion also enables us to see a certain symmetry in our discussions of intentionality, self-consciousness, and ethics. In each case, whether as inner speech, as feelings of being able to connect our contents with our context, or as objects of our intentions, contents have played some important role in the account. We may thus say that the one non-physical aspect of ourselves is richly connected to the main features of our "higher" mental life. The epiphenomenalistic character of contents does not mean that they can be ignored in explaining ourselves to ourselves. It would, however, be most unfortunate for this observation to become separated from the other main lesson of this book. Nothing can be accomplished by the postulation of simple relations of intentionality, simple selves, or simple ethical properties. In each case, the unavoidable price of real understanding is complexity; the minimum required unit, so to speak, is already a richly connected system of considerable size. Such complexity runs against persistent philosophical temptations to get fundamental matters down to very simple formulations. Against these temptations, one can only oppose the aesthetic value of seeing how a complex system produces a coherent result. I hope that I have been sufficiently clear about enough matters that this aesthetic value has begun to emerge.

INDEX

"Absent qualia" argument, 20

Acquaintance, 122–124

Adverbialism, 8–9, 11, 17, 149; similarity to Anscombe's view, 12–13; and topic neutralism, 13–16; and Levin's view, 159, 165

Afterimages, 11; as paradigmatic sensations, 3–4; properties of, 3–6, 34–35; adverbialist view of, 8–9; no characteristic related behavior, 13n, 19, 30n; thought experiments with, 14, 15; causes of, 26–27, 174–175; and reducibility principle, 32; as postulations, 33; not constituted by relations, 155; Levin's view of, 159–161; awareness of, 164–165

Anscombe, G. E. M., 10–13, 10n, 177n

Appearance-reality distinction, 58–59, 69

Appearances, 55–60

Armstrong, D. M., 25n, 60n

Attention, 177

Austin, J. L., 60n

Awareness, 11; of plurality, 152; Levin's view of, 161; of pain, 161–163; of afterimages, 164–165; Moore's view of, 170–172

Azimov, Isaac, 208, 208n

Behavior, 18, 20

Behaviorism, 19–23, 89–91, 143; and circularity problem, 90

Bergmann, Gustav, 83n, 119n

Block, Ned, 20n

Brentano, Franz, 88, 88n

Causes: and functionalism, 20–24, 30–31, 142–143; *vs* identity, 26–27; and evolution, 37, 39; and regularities, 40–42; and epiphenomenalism, 43–53; and "appearance", 57; and givenness, 66–67, 72, 75–79; and conditions for language, 97–98; and isomorphism of structure, 145; and independence of con-